Historical Commentary on First Corinthians

Also by William M. Ramsay

Historical Commentary on the Pastoral Epistles
Edited by Mark Wilson

Historical Commentary on First Corinthians

WILLIAM M. RAMSAY

Edited by Mark Wilson

Grand Rapids, MI 49501

Historical Commentary on First Corinthians

Published by Kregel Publications, a division of Kregel, Inc., P.O. Box 2607, Grand Rapids, MI 49501. Kregel Publications provides trusted, biblical publications for Christian growth and service. Your comments and suggestions are valued.

Cover design: Alan G. Hartman
Book design: Nicholas G. Richardson

Library of Congress Cataloging-in-Publication Data
Ramsay, William Mitchell, Sir, 1851–1939
Historical commentary on First Corinthians / Sir William M. Ramsay.
p. cm.
Previously "published in The Expositor, Sixth series, 1 & 2 (1900); 3 (1901)"—Introd.
1. Bible. N.T. Corinthians, 1st—Criticism, interpretation, etc. I. Title.
BS2675.2.R33 1996 227'.207—dc20 96-25512
CIP

ISBN 0-8254-3637-0

Printed in the United States of America
1 2 3 4 5 / 00 99 98 97 96

Table of Contents

Introduction

Ramsay's noteworthy status in biblical scholarship has been recognized by F. F. Bruce who, in the preface to his commentary on the Greek text of Acts, acknowledges, "My debt to the writings of Sir William Ramsay is evident throughout the work, and I am repeatedly amazed by scholars of a later date who seem unaware of the contributions of peculiar value which he made to certain areas of New Testament study."[1] From 1886–1911 he was Regius Professor of Humanity at the University of Aberdeen, his alma mater. His pioneering field work in Asia Minor advanced our knowledge of early Christianity and the Greco-Roman world. He was the author of nineteen books and scores of articles, including fifty-two entries in Hastings' four-volume *Dictionary of the Bible*. Best known among his biblical studies writings are the *Historical Commentary on the Galatians* and *The Letters to the Seven Churches*, which I recently updated (Hendrickson, 1994). The present volume follows Kregel's earlier publication of Ramsay's *Historical Commentary on the Pastoral Epistles*.

A challenge for Bible scholars and students today who seek to reference Ramsay is the inaccessibility of his writings. Most are out of print, and used copies are difficult to obtain from booksellers. Because of the datedness of his articles, few libraries contain the journals in their collections. Such is the case with the articles in this volume.

Ramsay first issued these fifty-one studies in a series called "A Historical Commentary on the Epistles to the Corinthians," published in the *Expositor*, Sixth Series, 1 & 2 (1900); 3 (1901). The entire series was never collected and published, thus this is the first publication of these articles in book form. Since the series in the *Expositor* failed to continue into 2 Corinthians, it was decided to limit the title of this volume to 1 Corinthians.

Editorial changes in the text have been minor. In the original series chapter 38 was mistakenly inserted too early as chapter 34.

This has been corrected in the book. Chapter 50, titled "Note on the Date of Second John," was moved to the Appendix because its topic was only incidental to the discussion of 1 Corinthians. Sentences have occasionally been modified for readability. Scripture references have been inserted to assist the reader, and Ramsay's original translation is maintained. Bibliographic information in the footnotes has been expanded when available and corrected when required. Finally, American spelling is used.

Special thanks must be given to Ellen Chappell for her faithful entry of the text, to Dieter Korr for his German translations, to Luwanna Baker and the interlibrary loan staff at Regent University Library for persistence in securing an original microfiche of the articles, and finally to Mike Bittel for the tedious task of making photocopies from the microfiche.

MARK W. WILSON

1

Introductory Remarks

In the following chapters it will be necessary from time to time to refer to the writer's *Historical Commentary on St. Paul's Epistle to the Galatians*.[1] It would be absurd to say again anything that is sufficiently said there, and the method which was gradually developed in the writing of that commentary will here be presumed from the outset. The same chronology also will here be assumed: this is not the place to discuss again the old questions that have already been sufficiently treated. Without desiring to force opinions on others, we have to assume the system which we think probable in points that lie outside of, but close around, our present subject.

It must also be clearly understood that, where theological or doctrinal points are touched upon, that is not done for their own sake, but for the sake of historical facts underlying them. The present writer has neither qualification nor wish to write on such points; but it is sometimes important to establish a date or some other part of history in connection with them.

Our main purpose is to estimate the light thrown by the epistles on the state of Corinth in the first century after Christ. Here we have a Roman *colonia* in the heart of Greece, capital of a Roman province, commercial and administrative capital of the whole country of Greece, containing a certain proportion of Roman population, descendants of the Italian colonists of 46 B.C., and a much larger proportion of purely Greek population. What can we learn about society in that great and wealthy and luxurious city on the great highway of imperial communication, a meeting place of many roads, thronged always by travelers and by resident strangers in addition to its own proper citizens?

2

The Contrast Between Galatians and Corinthians

The epistles to the Galatians and to the Corinthians were written at a short interval from one another. There is no reason to think that there was any change of the slightest importance in Paul's plans and methods during the interval. It is not as in the interval between Thessalonians and Galatians: during that interval, shorter though it was, there is good reason to think that Paul attained clearer consciousness about his method and order of placing his gospel before the Roman world. His gospel remained the same, but his plans for appealing to the Gentile world had become more fixed and definite.[1] But on the contrary, between Galatians and First Corinthians, there is no ground for imagining that Paul's views and method had altered a jot. Yet, amid a general agreement in the point of view, how profound is the difference between the two epistles!

The reason for this difference lies partly in the different character of the races addressed, and partly in the varying dangers to which they were respectively exposed.

The people of Galatian Phrygia and Galatian Lycaonia were essentially an Oriental race, with an admixture of the western element strong enough to serve as a model and a stimulus to the native population, and thus to affect them greatly, but not strong enough to change radically the people or to eliminate the Oriental spirit, but rather destined to melt into the native element.

The people of Corinth were a typically European people, familiar with every device and invention of an overstimulated civilization, essentially a worldly and material set of persons, seeking money and pleasure and success, excellent representatives of the worst side of rich "civilized" society, with little of the highest elements of Greco-Roman civilization.

In Galatia Paul had to deal with a somewhat backward race, but one recently touched and stimulated by contact with Greek art and literature, and with Roman organization and practical skill, a face naturally rather slow, simple, readily disposed to admire the bold and confident and educated foreigner. In Corinth he addressed himself to a people of diametrically opposite type, among whom a too prematurely developed civilization was entirely divorced from morality, a people keen-witted, pushing, self-assertive, conceited, highly trained, criticizing all people, questioning all things, not apt to believe in anything or anybody.

True religion has to steer a course equally far removed from the barbarism of primitive savagery and the barbarism of precocious material civilization. Christianity found the Galatians on their way up out of the former, and the Corinthians far on their way down into the latter.

Hence the contrast in many respects between the respective letters. Paul uses the tone of authority with the Galatians, of compliment and reasoned argument (though claiming official authority) with the Corinthians. He urges on the naturally self-willed Greeks the virtue of obedience, and on the "slavish" Phrygians the importance of freedom; he bids the Corinthians punish the violation of law, and warns the naturally "unpitying" Phrygians not to be too severe in punishing transgression. He loves the Galatians; he esteems the Corinthians.

Again, we observe everywhere that the difficulties and dangers besetting those early Gentile churches belong mostly to one or another of two classes. They spring either from the influence exercised by Judaism, or from the influence of pagan society and surroundings and early training. Every one of the Pauline churches was exposed to both kinds of danger; none were wholly free from either influence. But some were exposed more to the one kind, some to the other.

Among the Galatic Phrygians we saw that, when Paul wrote to them, the great and pressing danger lay on the side of Judaism: a part, apparently a majority, of the Galatian congregations were inclined to adopt the Jewish ritual. But that imminent danger did not blind Paul to the other danger that was equally pressing on them; and part of the later chapters is devoted to the dangerous influence of pagan society and religion and education.

In Corinth it was precisely the opposite. Paul's special purpose was to ward off the forces of paganism—chiefly in education and society—which threatened to unbalance and unhinge the constitution and morality of the church. Yet Judaism was also able to exert a dangerous influence in Corinth, and he had to turn his attention to that side also, especially in the second epistle.

But the grand difference between Galatians and Corinthians lies in the general character of the thought. The Galatian letter, when properly read, is found to be full of allusions to the practical facts of society and life, though from North Galatian misapprehension these facts are little noticed by the commentators. Paul explains to the readers his position and doctrines, and his attitude toward opponents, by illustrations drawn from the sphere of practical life. From that short letter we can restore at least some outline of the system of family law, of inheritance, of the external organization of education, of city life, and so on, familiar to Paul's Galatian readers. The attention of his readers must have been naturally turned more to that side of things; and Paul takes advantage of their special interests to put his ideas before them and to rouse in them the emotions and recollections which he desires.

In the Corinthian letters it is very different. A historical commentary finds much less to seize upon in them. They largely treat difficulties in practical life, and yet these are discussed from the speculative, philosophic, thinking side. Illustrations drawn from the external side of social organization are rare. Even where questions of society are referred to Paul's decision, he judges them so purely on general moral principles that we learn little about specially Corinthian society.

Here again we see the contrast between the Phrygian people, with its Oriental cast of mind, and the Greek race. This may seem strange and even self-contradictory to those who have not lived among these races, for business, trade, and skilled workmanship would seem to be the inheritance of the Greeks as contrasted with the Orientals—now and always. But one who comes in close contact with the Oriental villagers learns how entirely wrapped up they are in the matters of material life. You need never talk to them of ideal motives; they can neither conceive them nor believe in them. They know of no motive for action except a material one (apart from religious enthusiasm). But amid a group of the humblest Greek villagers, you are safe to talk of ideals, and you readily enlist their interest in them. In fact, unless you take them on this side, you will never succeed with them.

We have once more to repeat the remark that the right interpretation of Paul's epistles—Romans being a partial exception—must be founded on a vivid conception of the contrast between the Greek and the Oriental character, and of the eternal conflict between the two, which has always been going on in Asia Minor, and is now being waged there in a more marked and acute, and therefore more easily intelligible, form than at any previous time except during the early centuries of the empire. The two periods of acute conflict in that land, when the natural forces of society are struggling toward the establishment of a balance between themselves, and the realization of a higher form of expression, have been about 25 B.C.–A.D. 200, and since A.D. 1878.[2] The two periods ought to be always together in the student's mind; and we read in Paul's epistles to the churches the outlines of the ideal reconciliation between the Greek and Oriental nature in the borderlands, as he explained it to each in the way that they could most easily apprehend.

It is often asserted that a description of the Corinthian church is given in 1:26. That view we cannot accept. The context plainly shows that the verse is to be taken as a description of the Christian church in general, rather in contrast to rich, clever Corinth (see chapter 8).

3

Paul's Attitude to Judaism

A word is here required about Paul's attitude toward Judaism. It is absolutely necessary to bear in mind, though many are too apt to forget, that Paul was not an opponent of true Judaism. He could say to the end of his life with perfect truth and with a clear conscience, "I am a Pharisee, and a son of Pharisees" (Acts 23:6) and assert that he was "as touching the law blameless" (Phil. 3:6). He held fast to all the spiritual side of the law; he fully appreciated its moral elevation; he was (as we hope to show more fully elsewhere) throughout his life the great champion of the true law in the Roman Empire, and a firm believer in its ultimate triumph over the empire. But he hated the formalism, the dead works, of the law; and he fervently believed that in the law nothing except its formalism was opposed to Christ and that, when the law was set up as an opponent of Christianity among the Gentiles, the life had gone from it. It could not resist Him and live. When we read some of the harsh things said about the law, for example, to the Galatians, we are apt to lose sight of the fact that Paul is there speaking of the law as it appeared to the Galatians—as a series of hard and fast rules of ritual, as a system of observing days and months and seasons and years, as identified with belief in the moral efficacy of physical and bodily ceremonies. Paul would not even desire to abolish the mere ritual of Judaism. His action to Timothy, difficult as it is for us to sympathize with, proves that he would retain it. Only the most heartless and unprincipled of impostors could have acted as Paul did to Timothy, unless he were fully persuaded that the Jew must be always a Jew in the fullest sense, that he is always "a debtor to do the whole law" (Gal. 3:5). But Paul would prevent the Gentiles from incurring that debt.

It is not here the place to dilate more on this topic, still less to debate whether Paul was always philosophically consistent in his attitude to Judaism. But it is urgently necessary to protest against the too common exaggeration of Paul's hostility to Judaism. He certainly believed that he was the true friend and champion of his nation and his father's religion, and that his words addressed to the Sanhedrin were entirely consistent with his words addressed to the Galatians.

4

The Opening Address (1:1–9)

We can now better appreciate the special characteristics of the opening verses of First Corinthians. We take together the introductory address—the heading of the letter, so to speak (1:1–3)—and the opening paragraph (1:4–9).

Much in them belongs to the ordinary forms of politeness in letter writing. It was necessary and invariable to state at the beginning the names of the writer or writers and of the recipients of the letter, along with some courteous greeting and good wishes. Titles were commonly added to the respective names by the Romans (who were, to a large extent, the inventors of titles); then followed regularly an invocation or an expression of thanks to the divine power. In cases of haste or in unusual circumstances some of these polite accompaniments were often omitted.

Paul adopted the ordinary forms of epistolary courtesy, with similar occasional omission of some of the forms in special circumstances; only he gave a Christian expression to the titles and sentiments. On the subject see the remarks and references in *Historical Commentary to the Galatians*, chapter 5. Here we need only notice any details that are special to the Corinthian letter. These are three:

1. Sosthenes is named as joint author of the letter. It has been pointed out[1] that the occurrence of a name in the superscription of any of Paul's letters attaches far more importance to the person so mentioned than the sending of greetings from him at the end of the letter. It is extraordinary that this so obvious truth has been disputed. The case is exactly as when we find the superscription in a Roman letter.[2]

Balbus et Oppius salutem dicunt M. Ciceroni.

Both Balbus and Oppius take responsibility for the contents and sentiments of the letter, though probably one of them alone is responsible for the exact language. So Hellmuth points out with regard to the above letter, showing that Balbus is the author and Oppius merely the joint author.[3] So we have pointed out with regard to such letters as this.[4] Canon Evans has also stated the point with perfect accuracy and clearness in his admirable *Commentary on 1 Corinthians* (to which I am more indebted than to any other work on this epistle): "his name is associated to show that he shares, if not in the epistle" [that is, presumably its composition], "at least in the views and counsels contained therein, and endorses them."[5]

The superscription of the epistle is lengthened by titles and epithets from the simple form, which would be:

Paulus et Sosthenes Corinthiis salutem dicunt.

But the bare technical simplicity of Roman usage was alien to the warm and emotional nature of Paul.

2. He associates with the Corinthians "all that in every place call on Christ Jesus our Lord" (1 Cor. 1:2). The question has been much debated why this addition is made to the common type of introductory Pauline formulae, and many varying opinions have been maintained. On our principles of interpretation there can be no hesitation. The words stand in close relation to the burden of the letter. The Corinthians are in the process of losing unity. They have not yet split into religious parties and schisms; but Paul sees that the process has begun which, if unchecked, must result in that; and a great object of the epistle is to stop the process in its beginning. Hence he refers to the unity of the entire body of Christians.

A very similar thought occurs in the famous epitaph of Avircius Marcellus, written about A.D. 192 as a protest against the Montanist schism. The Phrygian saint lays great stress on the unity in feeling and practice which he had found prevailing everywhere from Rome to Mesopotamia.[6]

3. Paul compliments the Corinthians on their knowledge of truth and their ability to express it: "that you, namely, were in every way enriched in him, in all skill of discourse or argument, and in all kind of intelligence" (1 Cor. 1:4), as Canon Evans renders the words.

Gnosis, which is here the divine gift to the Corinthians, is apparently distinguished from *sophia* (which is spoken of so frequently in the epistle). *Gnosis* is the apprehension of the truth, that is, knowledge united with moral power to carry it into action. *Sophia* is the empty and powerless wisdom of mere verbal philosophy: add an idea and you have the true *sophia* of God, which Paul so often mentions.

Considering how severely Paul is about to inveigh against philosophy, and considering the character and interests of the Corinthian Greeks, it was peculiarly important to compliment them in this way at the outset. They have the true knowledge, and are advancing in it: why should they spend time and energy in empty philosophizing? The importance of this will become clearer in the sequel.

5

The Parties in the Corinthian Church

It is declared by the apostle that in Corinth "every one of you says, 'I am of Paul,' and 'I of Apollos,' and 'I of Cephas,' and 'I of Christ' " (1 Cor. 1:12). The attempt has been made by many commentators to specify the character of four supposed parties which used these four expressions as signs and badges of their respective views; but it may be doubted if the attempt has been made on the proper lines, or if it can be successful. Especially, as Alford says, "the German Commentators are misled by too *definite* a view of the Corinthian parties," and "much ingenuity and labour has been spent in Germany on the four supposed distinct parties at Corinth, and the most eminent theologians have endeavored, with very different results, to allot to each its definite place in tenets and practice."[1] Such attempts are on a radically false principle.

Let us rather attempt to determine in what way Paul conceived that the divisions arose. This he shows very clearly.

Perhaps the most obvious quality in the Greek race is its disposition to criticize and to argue. Paul makes it clear that the Corinthians had been fond of criticizing their teachers, of comparing them with each other, of discussing all their qualities and characteristics, of arguing about them.

Out of this quality arises factiousness: those who compared Paul favorably with Apollos joined battle with those who exalted the style of Apollos above that of Paul; and gradually the rival disputants were forming themselves almost unconsciously into factions, just as in later times the admirers of rival colors in the circus formed themselves into hostile parties. That is the fault which Paul regards as the fundamental evil in the Corinthians church, and sets himself at once to combat.

Hence he begins (1:10) by beseeching them all to speak the same thing, to have the same mind and the same judgment, that is, to be on their guard against the tendency to argue, to dispute, to see always the difference in their neighbors' views and remarks from their own, and never to have sufficient the agreement between them. As they discussed and criticized the teaching of their teachers, they almost came to maintain that Christ, as expounded by Paul, was different from Christ, as expounded by Apollos or by Peter, and that all three expositions of the Christ differed from the true idea of Christ.

It is obvious that Paul has in his mind a similar thought to that which is stated in Galatians 1:6–7, where he speaks of the "other gospel" preached by the Judaistic emissaries in Galatia. There he maintains[2] that, while the gospel set forth by the older and leading apostles may be called "another gospel," it is practically identical with his except when it is perverted by the errors of their would-be followers. We see elsewhere the evidence of the presence in Paul's mind of an idea that the Corinthians were too prone to see in the teaching of his successors "another Jesus" and "another gospel" from his (see 2 Corinthians 11:4).

But, as Paul declares in 1:13, Christ cannot be made into shares in that way, that is, it is the one identical Christ whom Paul and Apollos and Peter preach. If you consider that they set before you different Christs, then you are making Paul or Apollos or Cephas your Savior, and (if one may say so) believing that your special favorite, whether Paul or one of the others,[3] is your crucified Redeemer. The absurdity of their position is set forth in the indignantly ironical questions of 1:13, which are given as sufficient disproof. As soon as the Corinthians cease to say the same thing, and dwell on their differences of opinion, they go astray and "pervert the gospel" (as it is expressed in Galatians 1:7).

The third of these ironical questions is remarkable: "Were you baptized into the name of Paul?" This is coordinated with the other, "Was Paul crucified for you?" The Savior's death for them, and their reception by baptism into the name, are selected as the two great facts. The impossibility and absurdity of any teacher being put in Christ's place in these two relations is taken as too patent to need words. It is certainly a noteworthy point that these two ideas should be, as it were, bracketed together; but the importance lies in a direction foreign to our purpose and subject.

6

The Digression on Baptism

Here, in a very characteristic way, the allusion to baptism suggests to Paul a digression. He had rarely taken part in this office. He had baptized none of the Corinthians except Crispus and Gaius—Crispus, the former ruler of the synagogue in Corinth, and Gaius, who was deputed by the church to entertain all guests (a highly honorable duty in eastern lands, delegated to some distinguished member of the community). And then he recollects as an afterthought that Stephanas and his household were also baptized by him—perhaps Stephanas, who was with him in Ephesus as he wrote, reminded him—and so, to guard against any possible slip of memory, he adds, "Besides, I do not know whether I baptized any other"; but, if so, they were an insignificant number.

The rite of baptism Paul did not count as part of his work. There are diversities of gifts and ministrations, but all come from the same source (12:4ff.): "Christ sent me not to baptize, but to preach the gospel." Paul delegated this duty to his assistants and companions. He now expresses thanks to God that it had been so ordered that he had as a rule delegated to others this duty—a duty so important that his own performance of it might have caused misapprehension among the Corinthians.

7

Relation to Philosophy

This digression on baptism leads on to another. Paul has been led to affirm that his special duty and gift lay in preaching, and he again goes off to state emphatically the principle in his preaching. He had not trusted to philosophic argument, for to do so would be to distrust the power that lies in simply preaching the cross.

But this second digression brings him back to the original and main topic. The strength and at the same time the weakness of the Greek intellect lay in its acuteness, its capacity for making delicate distinctions and refinements, and its philosophic subtlety. The Corinthians shared in this Greek characteristic, and their habit of discussing and philosophizing about the doctrine of Christ was distracting their view from realities to unimportant distinctions. Just as it had led them to make that vain and dangerous distinction between the Christ of Paul and the Christ of Apollos and the supposed real Christ that lay behind them, till they forgot that Paul and Apollos and Peter were mere instruments of the one Christ, so also it prevented them from properly seeing and feeling the power that lay in the cross and in the simple preaching of the cross. While they discussed and criticized the style and the content of Paul's preaching, and subtly analyzed it, and delicately weighed its philosophic value, they lost sight of the one and only reality in it—the cross of Christ.

On this topic Paul enlarges at great length and from various points of view in chapters 1–4. In this theological discussion we notice only the following features, which suggest certain historical inferences.

1. Paul is continually striking at the philosophic vice of the Corinthians. They have not learned that the first step in the true philosophy is to strip from themselves every shred and scrap of their acquired knowledge, like Descartes in the beginning of his

Discourse on the Method of Using the Reason Aright. They must begin as bare as they came into the world, and build up their nature anew: they must make themselves babes, and grow into strength through weakness. They must cease to feel themselves to be philosophers, and recognize that they are fools, in order that they may be able to commence to learn. The beginning of true knowledge lies in the recognition of one's ignorance. Mere words of philosophic insight are absolutely inefficacious: the Corinthians must seek for that which has in it force and motive power, which can move the will: "for the kingdom of God is not in word, but in power" (4:20).

This state—the fully realizing and simply confessing of one's ignorance and natural incapacity—is called by Paul "folly," for to the clever Corinthians and the sophisticated person of the world it seems the character of a fool and a simpleton. But Paul only says all the more emphatically that a man must become a fool, a simpleton, in order that he may become wise (3:18): to become simple is the necessary and unavoidable first step on the road to the divine *sophia*.

On the moral side that same quality of "folly" would be the character that, from an innate rightness and healthiness, revolted against the impurity and frivolity of surrounding society, and declined to make pleasure, wealth, and power the absorbing aim and end of life. In the most corrupt state of Roman society we observe striking examples of this simplicity and purity, examples that gather luster and beauty in contrast to the worldliness around them, but which were liable to be ridiculed in refined and fashionable society as "folly."

2. Paul distinctly has in his mind, as he thinks of the Corinthian position, the Stoic paradox that the philosopher is everywhere sufficient for himself, always master of his circumstances—rich, powerful, free (though he be in prison or in a hovel), wise, everywhere king.

> Sapiens, uno minor est Jove, dives,
> *Liber, honoratus, pulcher, rex denique régum.*
> The sage is half divine,
> Rich, free, great, handsome, king of kings in fine.[1]

Throughout the epistle that thought recurs. The Corinthians "have knowledge." To them all things are lawful.[2] They are masters of their world. Especially, the thought gives point to the sarcastic contrast between them and the apostles (48 ff.): "Now you are full, now you are rich, you have reigned as kings without us[3]. . . . We are fools for Christ's sake, but you are wise in Christ; we are weak, but you are powerful; you are honored, but we are dishonorable." The thought which was stated in a complimentary way in 1:5, "You were enriched in all utterance and in all knowledge," is here given in a sarcastic form in 4:10, but the word changes from γνῶσις to φρόνιμος.

The same thought underlies the remarkable language of 3:21–22: "All things are yours, whether Paul or Apollos or Cephas, or the world, or life or death, or things present or things to come—all are yours." But here it is neither ironical, as in 4:8ff., nor complimentary, as in 1:5; it is the word of a seer and a mystic.

3. The most remarkable feature of the whole passage in chapters 1–4 is the ease and deftness with which Paul turns to his own purposes the ideas of philosophy. While he draws out in long detail the sarcastic contrast between the clever, able, and successful Corinthians, and the foolish, helpless, and hapless apostles, or between the grace and skill of Greek philosophy and his own humble, simple, unadorned preaching, he is really handling the deep topics of philosophy with a mastery that no other could have shown. And the most marvelous fact about the modern appreciation of these marvelous four chapters is that many commentators and writers take his sarcastic humility with perfect seriousness, and almost pity this wretched, uneducated, narrow, bigoted Jew, who has, "with stammering lips and insufficient tongue" (Isa. 28:11), to stand before the polished Greeks.

In truth Paul is here creating a Christian philosophy, and constructing a philosophic language to express it. It was not so difficult a task to make the Greek tongue express this new philosophic theology as it was 150 years later for Tertullian to re-express the Christian philosophy in the hard and intractable and anti-philosophic Latin, for Greek lent itself naturally and readily to the expression of high and ideal thought. But still it was by no means an easy task; and only a mind trained both in Greek philosophy and in Hebraic theology could have achieved it with the perfection that Paul has attained—a perfection so complete that the words become living, and brand themselves in the readers' hearts.

Paul is fully conscious of the nature of his task. He has to express the *sophia* of God (1:21; 2:7), that is, Christ who is the *sophia* of God (1:24, 30). So far is Paul from objecting to *sophia*; his special work is as much to set forth the true *sophia*, as to destroy the false *sophia*. He is the σοφὸς ἀρχιτέκτων, the philosophic architect, who lays the foundation for others to build upon (3:10). He has to create the language in which to express that true *sophia*: the *sophia* and the words in which to express it are both the gift of God: "We received . . . the Spirit which is of God, that we might know the things which are freely given to us by God: which things also we speak, not in words which human wisdom teaches, but which the Spirit teaches, fitting spiritual words to spiritual ideas" (2:12–13). So also, "We speak *sophia* among the mature; we speak the *sophia* of God, the divine system of true philosophy, the hidden scheme in which the intentions of God in the world find expression; and we speak it in the form of a mystery" (2:6–7).

To set forth that *sophia* was the work of Paul, the duty for which he was sent; and to that work he must necessarily devote his whole attention, leaving to others the work of baptizing (with all that was implied therein, much more than the performance of the ritual act), as we have seen in chapter 6.

4. Paul's severity towards Greek philosophy must not be misunderstood or exaggerated. It implies neither ignorance nor mere stolid resistance to education. One may inveigh against bad education, without being an opponent or depreciator of education. Just as to the Judaizing Phrygians of the province Galatia Paul inveighs against the evils and dangers of Judaic formalism, so here to the disputatious and sophistic Greeks of Corinth he inveighs against the evils and dangers of philosophic verbalism and juggling with arguments. But in regard alike to Judaic ritual and to philosophical education, there was another side to Paul's opinion, which is revealed in his life and work and in other parts of his letters. He held both that Jewish birth and blood implied the obligation to observe and practice the whole Jewish ritual (1 Cor. 7:18), and that the Christian must learn from the world around all that is best in that world.[4]

8

The Early Christians as a Part of Society

In attempting to understand aright the position and character of an early Christian community, we must be on our guard against the idea that all that was best in contemporary society tended toward Christianity. That was by no means the case. Those who were the most educated—in the best sense—those who were most refined and high-minded—those who were purest in life and aspiration—were often entirely content with their theories of the world and of the divine nature. And, in spite of the general corruption of pagan society, there were many striking examples of noble purity of spirit and life in the Roman Empire at the time when Paul was preaching.

In Roman official life, too, there were many admirable officers, devoted to their work, honest and incorruptible, with a splendid ideal of what a Roman official should be and should do.[1] It was by no means the case that these tended to become Christians. The routine of official life made many of them quite incapable of assimilating such new ideas as that men should think for themselves, and should refuse to accept the state worship which was the very essence and criterion of loyalty to the empire.

There were undoubtedly many of those early Christians who, taken in the naked reality of human character, were not equal in tone and spirit to many of the best pagans, and in themselves were incapable of rising to the same high level of life, or the same sanity and clearness of judgment. I am not thinking of mere hypocrites, who may have joined the church from mere selfish motives; there were such, we may be sure, even though Christianity offered little worldly inducement. The fire of persecution under Nero and Domitian and later emperors doubtless cleared the church of them, to a large extent, from time to time, though peace would always bring them back. But we cannot doubt that many of the genuinely devout Christians in Corinth and Ephesus and everywhere were very commonplace individuals. Some were naturally of low and vulgar nature in many respects. They represented the average, imperfectly educated stratum of ordinary society. They had by no means shaken off all the habits of thought instilled into them by pagan parents and surroundings when they became Christians. They required to be constantly watched, corrected, incited, guided, reprimanded, and encouraged. Their history was certain not to be a steady, uniform progress towards excellence: no human progress ever is so, except in the imagination of some theorists on religious history. There would assuredly be frequently a tendency among them to slip back into their old pagan habits and thoughts, to mix up old superstitions with new religious ideas. Some of them were quite unable to rise to the Christian ideal. Paul must often blame them for faults utterly unworthy of the religion they professed; and in this letter we find many proofs that much patience and much hopefulness were needed in treating the Corinthian church.

Paul gives a brief picture of the general social standing of the members of his churches in 1 Corinthians 1:26. This picture is not intended (as has sometimes been assumed) for a description of the Corinthian church specially, but we may safely assume that that church was not widely different from the other Pauline churches. In that passage Paul bids the Corinthians observe the principle that lies in the calling of Christians out of the world into the church. Not a large number of those whom the world counts its philosophers—not a large number from the official class clothed with the authority of the empire or of the municipalities—not many out of the old and aristocratic families—have been selected. No one within the church should plume himself in his advanced education or his official rank or his long descent, for though a few Christians possessed these worldly advantages, the reason of their calling lay not in those, but in very different qualifications.

This passage is often misinterpreted as proving that the early church was mainly drawn from the dregs of society. No such implication lies in it. To the historian the fact stands out clear that the work of the Christian church in society was to create or to enlarge the educated, the thoughtful middle class; and that those who were most suitable to form such a class were those who tended to drift towards the Christian church. Hence the church, when it was at its best, represented the force that stood in opposition, but in perfectly loyal opposition (as it always maintained), to imperial government, because the government claimed to think for its people as a parent for his infant children, while the Christians claimed to think for themselves.[2]

It is probably true that the class of freedmen and slaves was strongly represented in the church. But the freedmen, as a class, were set free because their natural ability and character had made them more useful to their masters free than as slaves. They were to a remarkable degree a moneyed class, and their money had been made amid great disadvantages by sheer force of character and conduct. As the same time they were also, as a rule, devoid of the higher education (which was almost entirely restricted to the free citizens), and as rich and uneducated and unpolished *parvenus*, they were often exposed to the ridicule of satirists and the contempt of the aristocratic and free born.

But they were also a class in which the average of ability and natural gifts must have been high; a class of self-made men, many of them possessing considerable aspirations, all of them endowed with much enterprise and energy—distinctly a vigorous stock. They were not separated from the free population around them by any obvious barrier of color and race, as were the emancipated black population in the United States of America. Hence the stigma of slave descent could not be permanently maintained through generations, and neither law nor custom tried to do so.[3] Yet this vigorous, able class rested under various disabilities and disqualifications, which rendered it an element of real danger to the state. Augustus, with his marvelous power of foreseeing and guarding against possible sources of disturbance in society, recognized and provided against this danger by creating a special sphere for the activities and ambition of that large class. A career was provided for freedmen, subordinate in character, yet opening to them distinctions, outward show, official dress and equipment, and abundant opportunity of gratifying vanity, and parading before the public eye their wealth and ostentatious liberality. And, like all Augustus' provisions, this special career was directed into the imperial service and worship, so as to attract the feelings of the whole class towards the person of the emperor.[4] But, like almost all the imperial arrangements, it had one serious evil. It appealed to the worse side of human nature: it tended to develop and employ the freedmen's energies on the side of personal vanity and empty show alone. It was absolutely without educational effect; it was killing to the loftier impulses, while it gave free play to the more contemptible qualities. It was part of the general imperial policy—food and amusements to the poor, dress and parade to the freedman—which, while it made them loyal at the moment, inevitably degraded and debased in the course of generations the tone of society in the empire.

The slaves who were attracted to the new religion were doubtless, for the most part, of similar type to the freedmen, and may be classed along with them. They were those who were on the way to earn emancipation.

The freedmen were, as a rule, engaged in trade and were, on the whole, a moneyed class. All of them, of course, used Greek as their ordinary speech in Corinth. The wealthy *parvenu* freedman was often satirized for his unsuccessful attempts to ape the manners of higher classes in society. In that Greek city he would imitate Greek fashionable society with a strain perhaps of Roman manners added, for the freedmen, as a body, owed their position to Roman law.

In Corinth the names Fortunatus and Achaicus (1 Cor. 16:17), and Gaius (1:14), probably indicate freedmen. Fortunatus was a characteristic servile name. Achaicus belongs to the class of geographical names, which (when not titles of honor bestowed on Roman conquerors) were commonly servile. Gaius was a *praenomen,* and the right to bear a *praenomen* was the distinguishing mark of freedom. Hence a freedman loved to be addressed by his *praenomen*, as Horace says:

> "Good Quintus," say or "Publius" (nothing endears a speaker more than this to slavish[5] ears).
>
> *"Quinte," puta, aut "Publi" (gaudent praenomine molles Auriculae).*

Gaius of Corinth, then, was probably a rich freedman, to whom the honorable duty of entertaining the guests of the church was assigned (Rom. 16:23). In his pagan days he would have aimed at the honorable position of a *Sevir Augustalis.*[6]

Another excellent illustration recurs to my memory. The freedman Gaius Pompeius Trimalchio in Petronius' *Satyricon* (which furnishes the only surviving picture of contemporary pagan society of the freedman class) is regularly spoken about and addressed, both by his household and by his friends, as "Gaius" simply. "Gaius Noster" was the name that pleased and flattered him. He was *Sevir Augustalis* at Cumae, and a leading personage there in his own class and set. The contrast between Christian and pagan society at this time could not be more strikingly and pointedly brought out than by a comparison between the two contemporary Gaiuses in the surroundings amid which each moved and lived. Petronius was writing only a very few years after Paul (earlier than A.D. 66), and he lays his scene about A.D. 47–57.[7]

Tertius (Rom. 16:22) and Quartus (v. 23) are also names which perhaps point to freedmen. In that case they would be actually names of slaves, who would retain them as *cognomina* after being set free. But they might equally well belong to provincials, especially resident strangers, not pure Greeks by birth, who settled in Corinth for purposes of trade.

The inference from these facts, and from the whole tone of the epistle, is that the church in Corinth contained a very considerable number of persons belonging to the well-to-do class of busy trades, many of whom were actually freedmen, some of whom probably were still slaves. But when we read of slaves, we are not to think of oppressed and degraded human chattels, like those of the cotton plantations in Mississippi before 1860, or of the similar class in the ancient *ergastula*, where the gang system was practiced on great estates, but of the household slaves and town slaves, well treated, on the whole comfortable, and enjoying considerable privileges according to an unwritten code of customs. These persons constituted, not indeed the majority, but certainly the strength, of the Christian community in Corinth.[8] And besides them there were also a few persons of the higher classes—philosophers, imperial or municipal officials (such as, at Athens, Dionysius the Areopagite). Around the church there was a fringe of persons interested, but not actually converts (such as the friendly Asiarchs in Ephesus, the proconsul in Cyprus, and so on).

To all these there must, of course, be added a large number of the really poor, the suffering class in society. There was plenty of opportunity for the well-to-do Christians in Corinth to exercise charity among their associates in the church as well as outside of it, and perhaps to plume themselves a little on their charity and virtue. But the tone of ironical admiration of the rich, clever, influential Corinthian Christians in chapter 4 loses all its effect if it is taken as addressed to a congregation of the poor and needy and humble only. It is addressed to persons who prided themselves not a little on their success in life and on the skill with which they had assimilated the manners of the most highly-educated and aristocratic classes.

Such was the Corinthian church; and as we have said, the other Pauline churches were not widely different. But this first Corinthian letter conveys a stronger impression of wealth and ease, and of the faults incidental to them, than any other of Paul's letters.

9

Sosthenes and Chloe

Sosthenes (1 Cor. 1:1) is a doubtful personality. The name was a common one; and Sosthenes of Corinth, who is mentioned in Acts 18:12, need not necessarily have been the same person. But if the two were the same, then certainly Acts would be found very illuminative of the epistle.

Sosthenes of Acts was a Jew of rank, still unconverted in the latter part of Paul's stay in Corinth; and if he is the Sosthenes of the epistle, he must have been converted, possibly by Apollos. His influential position in Corinth would be the reason why he is named as associate author of the epistle. If he were one of Apollos' converts, there would be special reason why he should be associated as joint author to stamp with his authority the warnings against criticism and faction.

We can, however, be certain only of one thing, namely, that Sosthenes, the author of the epistle, was a person known to the Corinthians, and standing in some position of authority as a teacher or preacher among them. Such was necessarily the case with an associate author of the letter to the Corinthians.[1]

Chloe (1 Cor. 1:11) is unknown. Nothing can be affirmed about her; and yet some probable inferences follow from the reference to her. We cannot suppose that Paul quotes the statement of messengers sent by one of the factious Corinthians as trustworthy evidence about the factions. It is clear that "the representatives of Chloe" are quoted as being in themselves good and sufficient witnesses, and therefore they must have stood outside the factions as external observers. Paul does not desire that Stephanas, Fortunatus, or Achaicus should be taken as his authorities. They were Corinthians, probably affected by the common fault of Corinthians; and it could only cause ill-feeling if they were understood to be his authorities. Chloe, therefore, was not a Corinthian. She was an outsider; and her representatives were unprejudiced witnesses in the matter.

Again, when we observe the important position of this woman, who was evidently head of a household, and perhaps of a business (like the Lydian woman from Thyatira at Philippi), we must recognize that Chloe was much more likely to belong to Asia Minor than to Greece. In Asia Minor, particularly in the less Grecized inner parts, women occupied a much more influential position than in the Greek cities.

Probably, therefore, Chloe was a native of some city of Asia Minor,[2] head of a business whose agents were passing to and fro between Corinth and Ephesus.

10

The Title "Corinthians"

It is noteworthy that Paul does not use the Latinized adjective *Corinthiensis*, but the simple *Corinthius*. In the case of Philippi, on the other hand, he uses the Latinized adjective *Philippensis*, Φιλιππήσιος in Greek.

Now it has been pointed out in chapter 25 (cf. also chapter 14) of my *Historical Commentary on the Galatians* what an important and characteristic feature is that use of the Latinized form of the adjective. It is exceedingly rare in Greek, and occurs only where the city is distinctively Roman and Latin. When Paul addressed the people of Philippi as *Philippenses*, he signified by this term that he regarded them as "men of a Roman *colonia*," Latins, not Greeks. We are reminded of the pointed description of Philippi in Acts 16:12 as a *colonia*; and we remember how many Roman features appear in the incidents narrated at Philippi.[1] Paul and Luke illustrate one another as usual. Each marks out Philippi as a city that prided itself on its dignity and its Roman character; and Paul, by addressing his converts as *Philippenses*, shows that he did not regard their pride in their own city, their *patria*, as either dead in their hearts after conversion or as wrong in itself. The address is strikingly analogous to that in Galatians 2:1, where the citizens of four cities in south Galatia are addressed as "men of the province Galatia."

But Paul does not address the Corinthians as *Corinthienses*; he writes to them as *Corinthii*. Both Corinth and Philippi were Roman colonies: why then the difference? Is it that he saw the church to be thoroughly Greek and not Roman? Or is it that the adjective *Corinthius*, not *Corinthiensis*, was in regular use in the city? The Latin adjective, in fact, seems to be known only from a quotation from the grammarian Festus, who mentions it as specially used to indicate a foreigner (or a Roman colonist) residing in Corinth. But all other evidence points to *Corinthius* as being the form used invariably by Romans; and the Latinized Greek form Κορινθήσιος seems never to occur.[2] Paul therefore probably followed the Corinthian usage, which was Greek, and the Philippian usage, which was Roman. That implies that Corinth had not become so thoroughly Romanized a place as Philippi; it was distinctively a Greek city, though a Roman colony.

We remember that in Acts 18 the incidents at Corinth do not have a strong Roman tinge. The presence of a Roman governor and his tribunal is a feature that belongs to Corinth, not as *colonia*, but as capital of the province. We find the purely Latin name Titius Justus and several other Latin names, especially of freedmen; but otherwise the local color is on the whole Greek rather than Roman. There is little to remind us that Corinth was a *colonia*, and its colonial dignity is not alluded to. Its rank as capital of Greece entirely outweighs its rank as a Roman city; and in the Bezan Text and the Textus Receptus the population are called "Greeks" in 18:17. This is an important point, deserving further notice. It has elsewhere been argued that the reading "Hellenes" is correct and necessary there;[3] and we shall now see how much meaning the term carries with it.

Here we notice that in Acts the term "Hellenes" (or "Greeks") is used with noteworthy propriety: the people of Thessalonica, of Berea, of Ephesus, of Iconium, and of Syrian Antioch[4] are spoken of as Hellenes. Those were all cities which had no claim to be Roman, except in the general way of being parts of the Roman provinces Macedonia, Galatia, and Syria. They were counted Greek cities, and reckoned themselves as such. But the people of the *coloniae* Antioch, Lystra, and Philippi are never called Hellenes. Even though in point of blood and rank and stock, the majority of the population were not Roman *coloni*, but Greek-speaking natives (who insofar as they had a Greek education and knew the Greek language were, according to the current designation, Greeks). Yet where the Roman idea was vigorous, these persons preferred to hear themselves designated as residents in a Roman *colonia* (or members of a Roman province), rather than as Greeks. The only doubtful *colonia* is Corinth, and in that case we see that Luke and Paul agree in thinking of it as the capital of Greece rather than the Roman *colonia,* and we can observe some probable good ground for that view.

This may seem a slight point; and some of my critics will perhaps ridicule me for dwelling so much on it. But it is precisely in such little details of custom and usage and politeness that truth to life can be judged.

There are, of course, at least two other uses of the word "Hellene" which must be distinguished from the above: (1) the generic contrast of "Jew and Greek," where "Greek" is representative of a class, and the antithesis is almost equivalent to "Jew and Gentile" and (2) the use of "Greek" to imply the non-Jewish blood and descent of an individual: Timothy's father was a "Greek" (Acts 16:1, 3) and Titus was a "Greek" (Gal. 2:3).

11

The Crime

Paul now proceeds to a crime which had been reported to him, and had roused his extreme indignation. One of the Corinthian Christians had taken to wife his stepmother. The circumstances are not described, because they were already known to the readers; and it is not easy to attain any certainty about them. From 2 Corinthians 7:12 it would appear that the father (assuming him, as seems inevitable, to be the "wronged man" there mentioned) was still living and known personally to Paul, and therefore presumably a Christian. On the other hand, the entire silence about the woman's conduct and about any punishment for her is hardly reconcilable with the idea that she was a Christian. If she were not a member of the church, her conduct did not fall under the cognizance either of the church or of Paul.

On the whole, then, it would appear probable that the pagan wife had separated from her husband, and that her stepson had thereupon married her. Any other supposition seems excluded by some of the conditions of the case. We notice that ingenious special pleading could set up some sort of defense or excuse for this action, which would not be the case in a more aggravated form of the crime (e.g., supposing it to have been brought about by the stepson tempting the woman to leave the father for the sake of the son).

It is evident that some such special pleading was possible in this case, and was actually practiced, for it seems implied without doubt that the Corinthian church was palliating the act and acquiescing in it. The Corinthians had not reported it in their letter to Paul. They had not asked his advice about it, yet they were quite aware of the circumstances (ἀκούεται ἐν ὑμῖν [5:1]), which were not concealed from the world. It must have seemed, therefore, to them to be a thing which concerned only the individual, and with which the church had no right or call to interfere.

The expression by which Paul indicates the blackness of the crime—"such immorality as [is] not even among the Gentiles"—has been misapprehended, as if Paul meant that such an act either was unknown or at least was universally disapproved among the Gentiles.

But it was not the case that such marriages were universally disapproved among the Gentiles. On the contrary, it must have been well within Paul's knowledge that marriages between even closer relations, and blood relations,[1] were regular and customary in eastern Asia Minor near his own city of Tarsus, and were widely practiced elsewhere.

Nor was it true that Paul is thinking of Greek and Roman feeling specially, taking those two peoples and civilizations as standing for "the Gentiles." Are we to suppose that the Corinthians had become laxer in their moral judgment when they adopted Christianity, and were now ready to condone an act which in their pagan days they would have regarded with horror? Or can we believe that Paul said so or thought so? I think not.

The real question that has to be answered is this: Would ordinary society in Corinth, or any other of the Greek cities of the Aegean coasts, have been shocked and outraged at a marriage between a man and the divorced second wife of his father? No one who has studied the state of Greek society will answer that question in the affirmative. Everyone knows that there was not in those cities such strictness of moral judgment. Greek custom and law had always been very lax as to restrictions on marriage. Marriage of uncle and niece, or aunt and nephew, had always been freely permitted in Athens. Stepbrother and stepsister might contract marriage with one another, if their relationship were through the father (though not if it were through the mother). When certain marriages are stigmatized as barbarian and offensive to Hellenic feeling (as, for example, in Euripides' *Andromache*), they are those of near relatives, alluded to above. It would be hard to find proof of any Greek objection to this Corinthian marriage even in the strictest period of Greek morality, if there ever was any strict period.[2] Certainly moral judgment was laxer in Aegean lands in A.D. 56 than in 450–400 B.C.

In short, the Corinthian church, when it condoned this crime, was simply judging as the Corinthians had always judged. It was not sinking below its pagan level. It was standing contentedly on that level.

What then does Paul mean? He is, beyond all doubt, referring to the Roman and imperial law, which (though not the immediate ruling law[3] in the Greek cities) was certainly known in a general way in the Corinthian *colonia*. He means, not that such a marriage was condemned by all Gentiles, but that it was condemned by the law which was most authoritative and supreme among the Gentiles—the law of the great empire.

Now Roman marriage custom was very much more severe than Greek. The old Roman laws had been extraordinarily strict in its prohibition of marriage between relations, forbidding even second cousins to marry one another. But the rule was relaxed by degrees. By the beginning of the second century B.C. marriage between first cousins had become legal and in A.D. 49 marriage between an uncle and his niece (if she were his brother's daughter) was legalized in order to admit the marriage of Claudius and Agrippina.[4] Again marriage with a stepparent or stepchild or parent-in-law was never allowed in Roman custom or law; affinity, in the direct line, always was a bar to marriage. Stepbrother and stepsister could never marry. This Corinthian marriage was, and always remained, illegal in Roman law.

The Corinthians, in practice, stood on the Greek level or moral feeling in regard to marriage; but Paul could count on the knowledge of Roman custom, which was to be expected in a *colonia*, even an eastern *colonia*.

12

Relation of the Corinthian Church to the Crime

The view stated in chapter 11—that the crime was a proof of failure to rise above the level of Corinthian pagan society and not of declension from the Greek standard—is entirely confirmed by Paul's language in the sequel. It is plain that, in the letter which the Corinthian church had sent to Paul, the crime was not mentioned.

The Corinthian officials (see chapter 13) had written to Paul a report of their present condition and prospects. So far were they from feeling any humiliation at the crime and any righteous anger at the criminal (such as Paul considered proper in the circumstances), that the report was full of self-gratulation. They felt how much they had gained by their conversion, how they had advanced in knowledge, in insight, in sympathy with divine things. They were full of hope, joy, confidence, and prosperity. They were "puffed up" (5:2)[1] and full of "glorying" (5:6).

The former of these two words is often in Paul's mouth during this letter: elsewhere he only once uses it (Col. 2:18). The second word and its derivatives express the idea that is most typical in both 1 and 2 Corinthians.[2] The tone of Paul's mind as he addresses the Corinthians is greatly determined by their attitude. As he faces them, the thought suggested to him is of persons rather presumptuously and dangerously self-confident and boastful; and he is continually talking of the false and the true grounds for glorying.

The Corinthians boasted of their prosperity, primarily of their spiritual prosperity, but also of their worldly success: the hand of God was with them and aided their enterprises. The paragraph in 4:6–13 and the references to their wealth, both the true and the false wealth,[3] show this clearly.

It is impossible to suppose that the Corinthian officials suppressed all reference to the crime from desire to conceal their own faults. That is not compatible with other evidence of their character and conduct. It is plain that they had no idea that there was any crime. Had the act been one which was beneath the standard of surrounding pagan society, the church must have felt that there was something about it requiring defense, and they would not fail to speak of it, to explain it, or to justify it. But their silence shows that they were quite unconscious of anything wrong about it. Their moral judgment remained, in this respect, on its old level, having neither seriously risen nor fallen. It is their callousness, their utter insensibility, that Paul rebukes.

It appears from 4:18 that one cause for the Corinthian self-gratulation was that Paul was not going to visit them a second time: "some are puffed up, as though I were not coming." This can only mean that a message had been sent, or an impression conveyed to them, that a visit from Paul was not needed–that the Corinthians were doing well, and could go on without a visit to confirm and strengthen them. We have already observed[4] that the repeated mention in Acts of visiting and thorough confirmation of the Galatian churches implies the strong need there was for strengthening those churches. And conversely Paul seems to have so put his previous letter (5:9, a lost letter), stating that he was not at present intending to visit Corinth, that this was felt to be a compliment to the strength of that church. We get the distinct impression that during his first two years' residence at Ephesus Paul had been receiving very good news from Corinth, but that at last bad news came to him and immediately called forth the epistle which we are studying. Timothy was already going to them by way of Macedonia. A letter also was now sent to them by special messenger (on the messenger see chapter 16); and Paul himself was coming (4:19).

It may be observed that this is the same procedure which, as we saw reason to understand, occurred in the case of the Galatian churches. Bad news came from them: Paul at once sent on a letter by a speedy messenger, and himself followed at a short interval. In the Galatian letter he did not so clearly intimate his intention of coming; but his expressed wish that he were now among them (Gal. 4:20) was supplemented by a verbal message.

13

Source of Paul's Knowledge of the Crime

In studying the difficult questions that arise in connection with the crime, we ask how and where he got his information about it.

As was stated in the preceding section, he did not get his knowledge from the letter of the Corinthian church; but he does not state who informed him. It is clearly shown in the epistle which we are studying that Paul derived information from at least three different sources; and the share of the different sources is marked out with unusual distinctness. Hence this epistle is specially valuable as a study in regard to Paul's sources of information, and his way of using them and referring to them. The situation is more clearly put in this epistle than in any other; but much that we see in it may be taken as applying to the others. Paul's sources here were three.

1. Information from third parties, travelers who were coming and going. These may without doubt be understood to be Christians: Paul was not likely to discuss with pagans the conduct of his own "children." In the constant lively intercourse that was going on between Ephesus and Corinth—two neighboring stations on the great route between East and West—he must have had many opportunities of acquiring information in this way. In some other cases he would not be likely to have such frequent opportunities. There would be far less intercourse between Corinth and Philippi than between Corinth and Ephesus. But traveling was wonderfully common, easy, and certain at that period. Until a very recent time there has never again been in Europe anything comparable to the means and frequency of travel under the Roman Empire. To this class belonged the representatives of Chloe (1:9).

2. Paul had received from the church at Corinth an official letter, reporting good progress and success, asking his advice on various

practical questions, stating the opinions held in the church, and urging certain arguments. We shall find frequent references made to this letter, and quotations from it; for Paul often quotes Corinthian opinion before he corrects or completes it. His advice often must be regarded in the light of their opinions and arguments before we can properly understand it. He did not require to advise them to do what they were already doing rightly. He directs his advice towards the subjects in which they have to be corrected. Unless this is borne in mind, his advice would sometimes appear one-sided.

A single letter taken apart from a continued correspondence must always be difficult to comprehend. The receivers are on the outlook for a reply to their questions and arguments. They catch the retort which depends for its effect on their own previous statement. Much in Paul's epistle is obscure for that reason; and we must always be on the outlook for any hint as to the character of the letter which the Corinthians had sent him.

We shall be ready to suspect quotation, in the first place, when an idea recurs over and over again without being one that is obviously and characteristically Pauline—such are the allusions to knowledge, to the freedom which knowledge confers to do all things, to wealth, to boasting and being puffed up—and in the second place, where any statement stands in marked contrast either with the immediate context or with Paul's known views.

The letter from Corinth was brought by three messengers—Stephanas, Fortunatus, and Achaicus—who are marked out by their names as probably freedmen and men of business (see chapter 8). It is not necessary to suppose that they were sent for the express and single purpose of carrying the letter. It is much more in keeping with ancient custom that some or all of them were going on business to Ephesus, and were entrusted with the letter. This mission gave them additional honor and importance. The Greek cities often employed such envoys (πρέσβεις) to Rome, using their services and so economizing expense. The envoys were rewarded with a public inscription recording their services and with the increased dignity at the time.

We may confidently assume that the letter was composed by the officials of the church. There was not yet, apparently, a single *episkopos*; and the *presbyteroi*,[1] or a small committee of their number, would most probably be charged with the duty. The view has been stated elsewhere that the institution of a single *episkopos* was due in considerable degree to the importance and necessity of maintaining the unity of the entire church by constant intercommunication between the scattered parts. A letter, in the last resort, is likely to be mainly the composition of one man.

Considering the character and institutions of a Greek city, we need hardly doubt that the letter was finally submitted to the approval of the entire *ekklesia* or church. But this probably was merely for acceptance or rejection, for no amendment or discussion was now permitted in the meetings of the whole body of citizens under the empire, while the Christian *ekklesia* may be assumed to have felt entire confidence in its directors, and to have forthwith endorsed their composition.

3. The envoys who were honored with the duty of bearing the letter were doubtless charged with many verbal messages, and would give a report to Paul of the state of the community. This would be understood by the whole church at Corinth; and where Paul mentions any fact which was not in the letter, the Corinthians would naturally presume that Stephanas and the others were his informants, unless he expressly mentioned some third party.

We must, therefore, conclude that the envoys gave Paul the information which called forth the strong language of the fifth chapter. Probably they showed themselves as unconscious of the serious nature of the crime as the other Corinthians were, and exemplified that lowness of moral standard which Paul rebukes.

14

The Judgment of Paul

After censuring strongly the laxity of the Corinthian judgment on the crime (5:2), Paul contrasts their indifference with his own severe judgment (vv. 3–5). This remarkable passage is a striking example of the difficulty that the modern reader must sometimes experience in attempting to understand the thoughts of the first century. It plunges the reader into circumstances and ways of thinking which it is hardly possible for him to comprehend, and he is apt to interpret the passage by reading into it the ideas of a later time. Some serious misconceptions of it can be cleared away; but we may despair of being able ever fully to understand the meaning that it bore either to the writer or to the original readers.

The exact words are so important that they must be quoted in full: the form differs a little from the Revised Version. "For I, at any rate, being absent in body but present in spirit, have already, as if really present, formed the decision in respect of him that has so wrought this thing, in the name of the Lord Jesus, you being gathered together and my spirit, in association with the power[1] of our Lord Jesus, to deliver such a one unto Satan for the destruction of the flesh, that the spirit might be saved in the day of the Lord."

1. This passage must be connected with the preceding verse, not with the following. The particle μέυ, with which it opens, is not here to be understood as pointing forward to a following δέ, (understood or expressed): we must take μὲν γάρ together and "connect with the last verse."[2] It expresses the contrast between the attitude of the Corinthians and the attitude of Paul toward the crime.

2. This passage has been frequently interpreted as describing a formal judicial decision and sentence passed on the offender in the most solemn and awful fashion. So far as I have observed, that grave and solemn sense is universally taken from the words: they are read as carrying with them excommunication and worse, or

even, as some say, a miraculous punishment. The fact that here Paul speaks without consulting the Corinthian officials has even been regarded as a proof that they had no power in the matter, but that Paul alone, without their presence or assent, was empowered to judge and decide and condemn the guilty person to the extremest penalty both spiritual and physical, merely intimating to the church the sentence which he had passed.

Any such view can hardly stand the test of reasonable consideration.

1. It supposes that Paul judges and condemns on mere hearsay evidence—evidence of whose nature he gives the church no account—without hearing any defense, without giving the accused party any intimation that he is being tried. Such a parody of justice could be paralleled only by the very worst acts attributed to the Inquisition in its worst period.

2. The supposed sentence of excommunication, and worse than excommunication, remained a mere *brutum fulmen*, which was never put in effect. The church in Corinth judged the case, and decided on a much milder sentence, which Paul entirely approved (see chapter 16).

3. Paul does not here represent himself as pronouncing a formal sentence. He continues his remarks in a tone so different as to constitute an extraordinary anticlimax, if the decision and sentence were already pronounced. He discusses the principles involved in judging such a case (assuming that the Corinthians will judge it). He concludes in 5:13 by quoting from Deuteronomy 24:7 the sentence to be pronounced on the man who is found guilty; and the sentence is very much milder than that stated in 5:3–5. But it is merely irrational, and unjust to Paul, to suppose (as some practically do) that he first expresses in violent anger too strong a sentence, and then cools down so far as to demand a much milder punishment a little later.

Henry Alford sees that 5:3–5 does not actually convey a formal sentence, and interprets it as "a delegation to the Corinthian church of a *special power, reserved to the Apostles themselves, of inflicting corporal punishment or disease* as a punishment for sin."[3] But there is no word in 5:3–5 that suggests delegation of Paul's power to others: there is merely a statement of Paul's own opinion.

The clue which must guide us is the grammatical construction. We saw that 5:3–5 is to be connected with 5:2. Paul contrasts the indifference of the Corinthians with his own vehement condemnation, not of this man, but of any such person, that is, any person guilty of such conduct as has been attributed by rumor to this man.

This is not a case for inaction: it is a case for instant action, but action according to the rules of justice and moral principle. The lazy, contented, self-satisfaction of the Corinthians must be sharply checked.

The words "I have judged him" (κέκρικα), then, do not imply a legal judgment, but an expression of Paul's opinion on a mere report of the case. It is the first step, as it were, in a legal case: the matter has been reported, so to say, to the *praetor*, and he decides that there is a case, and sends it for investigation before the proper tribunal, stating the severe view which the law takes of such cases, if proved.

3. What exactly does Paul mean, and what did the Corinthians understand him to mean, by the terrible words in which he expresses his opinion? Here I confess my inability to decide. It is a case where the habits and ways of thought in another time and amid another people are peculiarly hard to understand or to sympathize with. But we must try at least to place before ourselves some analogous cases.

The expression "to deliver such a one unto Satan" is also employed by Paul in 1 Timothy 1:20 about Hymenaeus and Alexander, who had made shipwreck concerning the faith, "whom I delivered unto Satan that they might be taught not to blaspheme." But the circumstances there are too obscure to afford any help in the present case.

A path which at least seems promising—though possibly the appearance is only deceptive—is to inquire what meaning the Corinthian readers would attribute to the words. They had been accustomed in their pagan life to very similar formulae, in which a person who had been wronged by another and had no other way of retaliating, consigned the criminal to the god, and left the punishment to be inflicted by divine power. These forms played a great part in ancient life, and many examples of them have been preserved to our time. We find divine wrath and punishment thus invoked against thieves, slanderers, poisoners, assassins, an adopted child who had raised his hand against his foster mother, users of false weights, persons who refused to restore money deposited in their case, and so on. Even a mere advertisement of lost property was accompanied commonly by a curse consigning to divine punishment anyone that found and did not restore the lost article.

In such cases the sufferer, who entrusted his vindication to the divine power, was said to make way for the god as his champion.[4] The god was conceived as a judge, whose power was set in motion by this formal supplication. We know of such actions in two ways—

sometimes from the invokers of divine aid who wrote out and left at the temple a formal statement of their appeal with the reasons for it,[5] and also regularly commemorated by a dedication and inscription the aid that they had received and the punishment inflicted on the wrongdoer—sometimes from the wrongdoer who, when punished, recognized his fault and dedicated an inscription (accompanied doubtless by a gift), confessing his sin and glorifying and propitiating the divine power which had punished him.[6]

In these invocations the god was asked or tacitly expected to punish the wrongdoer by bodily disease. Fever—in which the strength wastes through the effect of "subterranean fire" without special affection of any part—was regarded as the favorite weapon of the god; but any bodily affliction which came on the accursed person was regarded, alike by the invoker and by the sufferer, as the messenger or weapon of the god.

The Corinthians who read Paul's judgment in 5:3–5 could hardly avoid interpreting it by the analogy of that pagan custom, which had been familiar to them and doubtless often practiced by them until about two or three years before. Even yet they were not very far removed above the old pagan level. One must ask the question, Would they not take Paul's judgment as a Christianized form of the pagan usage? The criminal is handed over to Satan (who, however, is here treated as the instrument in divine hands); and if there subsequently befell him any bodily suffering, it would be regarded as the divine act to the end that he might repent and learn.

15

Principles in Judging the Crime

Paul proceeds to point out two important considerations which must be taken into account by the Corinthian church in judging this case.

1. "A little leaven leavens the whole lump" (5:6), as the proverb is. One sin and one sinner, if regarded with indifference, may ruin the whole Corinthian church. The old leaven of their pagan ways must be completely cleared out, and they must devote themselves to Christ, to live his life.

The allusion to leaven, at first a mere figure of speech, leads Paul to work out the figure into an allegory. If sin is the leaven, then Christ is the Unleavened, and the life of Christ is the Unleavened Feast. And we Christians ought to keep the feast and live the life in all perfection and purity (5:7–8).

It is unjustifiable to find here an allusion to the season of the year when Paul was writing, as if the celebration of the Passover at the moment suggested to him the comparison of Christ with the unleavened Passover bread. As we see, that comparison is suggested by the proverb which he quoted in 5:6.

Moreover, if Paul had been giving instructions to the Corinthians as to how they should celebrate the Passover, he would have done so beforehand, and not in a letter which could not reach them until the feast was ended. It is probable that Paul did write this epistle in the end of winter or the early days of spring, and that 11:18–34 and 10:1–11 were written with a view to the coming Passover of the year 56 (Friday, March 19, according to Lewin).[1]

2. Christians must not associate with immoral persons. Such was the instruction given by Paul to the Corinthians in his previous letter; he now explains (evidently in reply to some criticism on their part), that the rule[2] must not be taken in the sense that they

should exercise a censorship over their pagan neighbors (5:12–13), and refuse to meet them in society.

The tone of society and the code of morals in pagan cities were of so low a standard that, if the Christians carried out that extreme principle, they would have to go out of the world altogether. But it was always part of Paul's teaching that his converts should not retire from the world, but should live their life in the state, and try to conquer the world around them. The Corinthian church should confine its judgment and censorship to its own members. But within its own bounds it must exercise strict supervision, maintain a high standard of morality and conduct, and expel any unworthy member. Christians must refuse all intercourse with a Christian who has sunk from (or failed to rise to) the necessary standard of Christian morality. They must not even eat in his company: this implies that they are not to invite him or accept his invitation, but not that they are to go away from any society in which he appears (for that is covered by 5:10).

Such are the chief principles involved in judging the crime; and the judging of it is a duty that must be discharged.

16

The Result

It would be interesting to know what was the issue of this case. The references which are made to it in 2 Corinthians are too vague to show exactly what occurred, but they throw some light on the progress of the case.

It was probably not very long after sending off this letter to Corinth that Paul left Ephesus. He had intended to remain there till Pentecost was past, but the riot of some of the trades connected with the temple forced him to leave prematurely. He was at this time feeling very anxious and despondent about the Corinthians, as he says in the opening of 2 Corinthians; and this feeling lasted through his stay at Troas, where he went after leaving Ephesus. He expected to meet Titus in Troas with news from Corinth; but in this he was disappointed, and his anxiety drove him on to Macedonia, where he found Titus and was cheered with a good report.[1]

Titus was able to assure him that the Corinthians had been deeply touched and stirred up by Paul's letter. Their insensibility to the serious nature of the crime had disappeared; they realized its true nature and were full of sorrow and of repentance. They apologized for their conduct, explaining how they had only failed to see clearly, but had not willfully erred. They were eager to judge the case and to punish the offender (2 Cor. 7:7–11).

But now a new consideration came in. The offender had been as unconscious of the crime, and as free from deliberate intention to err, as the rest of the church. He proved this by the profound sorrow and humiliation which he felt. In those circumstances, when the trial was held, the sentence inflicted was not so severe as Paul had indicated. But clearly this result was not unanimous; a minority were of opinion that they should implicitly obey Paul and inflict the full sentence.

This situation was reported by Titus; and Paul replied (2 Cor. 2:6–10) that the punishment inflicted by the majority was sufficient, and a severer one was not required, as suggested by the minority.[2] They should now feel able to forgive and console the offender, lest in his humiliated position he might despair and "be swallowed up with his overmuch sorrow" (v. 7).

Paul had regarded this as a case testing whether the Corinthians were obedient (2 Cor. 2:9); that is, probably obedient to God rather than obedient to Paul. Now he knew that the Christian idea was raising them gradually to its level. He cordially accepts their decision, and forgives him whom they forgive.

Incidentally we remark that it is hardly possible to avoid the conclusion that Titus carried to Corinth Paul's letter (1 Corinthians)[3] and was to bring back an answer and to report on the case. Then, when Paul had to leave Ephesus suddenly, he must have sent a message to Titus bidding him come round by the coasting voyage to Troas. Finally, when his arrival was delayed, Paul went on and met him in Macedonia, perhaps at Neapolis, the harbor of Philippi.

17

Litigation in the Corinthian Church

The subject of chapter 6 had evidently been suggested, not by a formal question addressed to Paul by the church,[1] but by some information which reached him. For the reasons already stated, we may assume with every probability that the information came to him through Stephanas and his two companions (see above in chapter 13). From them Paul learned that it was usual among the Corinthian Christians to take legal action against one another in the ordinary pagan fashion, with pagans to decide the points at issue, and that public feeling in the church did not regard such procedure as unsuitable or unbecoming.

As before, the fault of the individual here springs from the tone of the Corinthian church in general; and Paul's remarks are directed more to produce a healthier tone in the community as a whole than to rebuke the action of individuals. In fact, his expression in 6:1 is put in such general and vague terms as to leave it uncertain "whether any particular case was in the apostle's mind at the time."[2] Dare any of you, having a matter against his fellow Christian,[3] go to law before the unrighteous (i.e., the pagans) instead of before the saints, the Christians?

Paul's words have not been correctly understood by most commentators. Some seem to think that he orders the Corinthian Christians to appeal to church courts instead of to the ordinary courts of law. But that is quite out of keeping both with his language here and with the whole tone of his teaching. He never expresses disrespect for the established institutions of the country and the empire, or advises that the church should create a rival organization. He always teaches his converts to accept and make the best of existing institutions.

Others think that the alternatives in 6:1 are different in character, and that the process before the Christians would be in the form of arbitration, while before the heathen it would be according to the legal forms then prevailing. But the expressions describing the two alternatives are so exactly parallel—κρίνεσθαι ἐπὶ τῶν ἀδίκων καὶ οὐχὶ ἐπὶ τῶν ἁγίων, where both pagans and Christians are designated by terms expressive of moral and religious character—that we cannot fairly think they describe different processes.

Paul here is not thinking of serious questions of crime and fraud so much as of the small matters, which persons of a litigious character—such as the Greeks were—are always ready to make into causes of disagreement and legal action. Now such small cases were ordinarily decided in Greece by umpires or arbiters chosen by the parties themselves. The expressions used throughout the passage suggest rather informal proceedings than formal trials on legal principles before judges (δικασταί). The terms used are κρίνω, κρίνομαι, κριτήριον, and κρίμα, all of which are appropriate to cases tried according to the least strict procedure by umpires whom the parties select (αἱρετοὶ κριταί, διαιτηταί), and who decide, not according to formal written law (νόμος), but according to their own conception of right and wrong.

That Paul is not here thinking of serious and grave matters is clear from 6:4, where unfortunately the Revised Version is far from good. (1) The subjects brought up for decision are called "matters of everyday life" (βιωτικά),[4] the trumpery details of common life, which afforded many opportunities for the Corinthian Greeks to quarrel about prices and ownership and so on. (2) The litigants set any persons they please as arbitrators to judge the individual cases;[5] the place where the arbitrator takes his position becomes the κριτήριον; the proceedings are *ex tempore*. Nothing suggests the "public arbitrators," who were chosen by lot in Athens by the magistrate in court from the permanent *daitetai* (κληρωτοὶ διαιτηταί).

Some commentators, who insist that Paul is here referring throughout to formal legal procedure before courts of law, maintain that the word κριτήριον in 6:2,4 means "courts" or "tribunals." That is inconsistent with 6:4 (βιωτικὰ κριτήρια ἐὰν ἔχητε), where the nominative is the litigating parties—"If you have matters of common life to set before a *krites* for decision, select as arbitrators persons of no account in the church."

But, Paul proceeds in 6:7–11, it is quite a fault in you to find provocation to suits among yourselves. You ought rather to acquiesce patiently in (what you consider to be) unfair treatment or inadequate recognition of your rights. And along with that fault there always goes the other fault of unwillingness to recognize adequately the rights of others: "you yourselves act unfairly and defraud, and that your brothers" (6:8). In the preceding paragraph I bade you refuse to associate with anyone guilty of crime (5:11). Now I remind you that all such are rejected by God. Those are the sins and faults of your former pagan life; and in your new life you ought to have risen above them.

The fault to which the Greek nature was and is most prone is that which Paul calls πλεονεξία (rendered "covetousness" generally in the Revised Version[6] and identified with "idolatry" in Colossians 3:5), the tendency to insist on getting at least one's full rights, and therefore often even more than one's fair share. Carried to an extreme and combined with a low moral standard of action, it becomes that grasping, greedy, cunning kind of dealing. But even with a higher spirit and principles, the fault is not eliminated, and the Corinthian Christians had not shaken themselves free of it. They still, in their mutual dealings, were apt both to think that others were denying them a fair share, and in their eagerness to get their full portion, to claim more from their neighbors than they had a right to.

In this passage it is clear that Paul is thinking rather of Greek than of Roman procedure. A similar custom of using and choosing umpires to decide small cases existed originally in Rome; but in the more developed Roman procedure the umpires (*judices, arbitri*) were appointed by a magistrate, and even very simple cases involved a stage of formal legal procedure. Such was the almost universal rule under the empire wherever procedure was of the Roman type. But, as has elsewhere been pointed out,[7] the Romans never tried to force their own system of law and society on the eastern provinces, which had an old-standing civilization of their own; and doubtless even in Roman *coloniae* in the east, procedure in unimportant civil cases was more Greek than Roman in the time of Paul.[8] Just as in south Galatia we found that the law presupposed by Paul's letter seemed to be of the Seleucid type (i.e., Greek modified by the conditions of an Oriental kingdom), so in Corinth we see that the law in private cases is of the Greek, not the Roman, character, freer and less formal. The people of Corinth would be likely to know more than most Greeks about Roman imperial law in great matters (see chapter 11); but the ordinary life of the city at this time was evidently Greek rather than Roman (see chapter 10).

18

Sequence of Topics in Chapters 5–7

It is characteristic of Paul that often, while treating one subject, he already has the following topic in his mind, and in the treatment of the first he is preparing and paving the way for the next. Thus he passes from one to the other, and even returns to the first after or during the discussion of the second. Every one of his epistles has an extraordinary unity, as of a living body. Each topic seems to be vitally connected with every other, and they melt into one another, so that the reader feels he cannot treat the epistle except as a single organism where every part must be studied before any one is fully comprehended. Galatians is the most striking example of this; but all show the same characteristic.

The first epistle to the Corinthians treats a far greater number of separate and distinct topics than any other of Paul's letters. Much of it is in answer to a series of disconnected questions addressed to him; and along with these are included a number of topics suggested to him in other ways. Yet the epistle holds these various topics together by a bond of unity. It becomes a unified whole; and the unity lies in the strong, overpowering, determining idea in Paul's mind of the Corinthian nature and needs. The epistle has the unity amid variety of Corinthian church life as Paul saw it.

A good example of this is seen in chapters 5, 6, and 7. In chapter 5 the subject is a certain serious crime committed by one of the members of the Corinthian church; in 6 it is the litigiousness of various members of that church, and their fault in bringing their cases for decision by pagans; in 7 the topic is marriage, celibacy, and immorality. But in 5:12–13 the duty incumbent on the church of judging the crime is mentioned in such a way as to slide into the topic treated in 6, while 5:9–11 touches the topics of 7 quite closely as they do the main topic of 5. Again, 6:9 glides into a subject preparatory to the topics of 7 (which were already foreshadowed in 5: 9–11), and 6:12–20 discuss that subject at length.

19

Judging the World

When we take these parts together, it is apparent that a certain discrepancy arises between 6:2–3 and 5:12–13. In 5:12–13 Paul declares that the church has nothing to do with judging the outer world: it judges its own members and expels the unworthy from its midst, and it leaves the outer world to the judgment of God. But in 6:2–3 he asks, "Do you not know that the saints shall judge the world? And if the world is judged by you, can you not find among your fellow Christians persons worthy to judge the insignificant matters of everyday life about which you dispute before heathen arbiters? In reality, you should choose the humblest members of the church to arbitrate in those small matters."[1]

But the passage in 6:2–3 is not entirely serious. In 6:4–5 the apostle goes on to say that they ought to choose those who are of no account in the church to act as arbiters in such insignificant matters, which are unworthy to occupy the time and attention of more important members of the church. And then he explains that he "says this to move you to shame"; his words are not to be taken as serious advice. The undertone of sarcasm, almost of banter, is to be understood as ruling throughout 6:2–4.

This becomes all the clearer when we remember the principle already laid down (see chapter 13), that we should be ready to suspect Paul is making a quotation from the letter addressed to him by the Corinthians whenever he alludes to their knowledge, or when any statement stands in marked contrast either with the immediate context or with Paul's known views. These criteria mark 6:2–3 as an allusion to some very self-satisfied expressions in the Corinthian letter: "Of course, you know that the saints shall judge the world, and even angels (Is it not written in your letter?)."

The commentators who take 6:2–3 as a serious description of the future powers and duties of Christians are hard pressed to find any really satisfactory explanation of the words as expressing a principle to which Paul attached any importance. Anyone who works out for himself a connected conception of Paul's views about the place of man in God's universe must either tacitly leave out of sight those two verses, or must say, as we do, that they are not to be taken as a serious philosophic enunciation. It is usual among those who take 6:2–3 seriously to quote Matthew 19:28 and Luke 22:30 in illustration. But those passages only show how impossible it is to attach any serious importance to this one, though they may have been in the mind of the Corinthians when they wrote the sentences which Paul is quoting or alluding to.

20

Purity and Immortality (6:12–20)

Throughout the letter Paul has before his mind a clear picture of the general position and difficulties and surroundings in which the Corinthian church was situated. He is never so occupied with any of the details which he successively takes up, as to lose sight of the bearing of each on the general state of the congregation. He sees that the prime necessity is to raise the general standard of moral judgment; and that the correction or punishment of isolated errors and crimes can do little good until the church as a whole is placed on a higher moral level. Some members of the church, at least, had been criminals of the worst kind in their pagan days (6:11), not so very long past; and though they have washed themselves[1] and been sanctified, yet the past habit and the pressure of surrounding society make a serious and continual danger.

Especially was the danger great in the direction of purity of life; and to this subject Paul returns time after time. The obligation to a pure life must be constantly urged on the Corinthians. The frankly confessed and universally held theory on the subject in pagan society was that every requirement of the body was in itself natural and right and ought to be satisfied fully and healthily in whatever way and time and manner the individual found convenient, the only standard applicable for judging the individual's conduct lying in considerations of physical health and beauty. The same principle was applied to purity of life as to food and nourishment: in neither case was there any standard according to which the conduct of people should be judged except consideration of the physical health of the individual. So long as any action was pleasant to the individual and did not injure in any way his physical well-being, it was right.

Against this theory, accepted in all pagan society and perhaps not quite obsolete in the church at Corinth, Paul argues in the paragraph before us; and his argument is that of a mystic. It is true that the standard of judgment as regards feeding is purely one of physical health and beauty (6:13); but food and the body as an organ for assimilating food are alike transitory and perishable. On the other hand, the body as a vehicle of life and spirit is eternal and imperishable; and its proper function in this respect lies in its relation to God, not in individual satisfaction.

This doctrine must be taken in connection with the teaching of chapter 15 on the immortality of the body. The physical body is not immortal, but the body as spiritual is immortal. Purity of life is in the closest relation with the spiritual character of the body, and is the prime condition of spirituality: other sins do not affect the spiritual nature of the body, but impurity destroys it (6:18).

The doctrine is also closely connected with Paul's conception of true marriage as the most perfect symbol of the relation between Christ and the church, between the divine and the human life (see Eph. 5:23, 29–30); and thus the paragraph before us forms the natural transition to the subject of chapter 7 (according to the custom of Paul; see chapter 18).

That the outspoken naturalism of the pagan theory against which Paul argues was not entirely abandoned in the Corinthian church is perhaps proved by his opening words in 6:12: "All things are lawful to me," as you say in your letter, but one should add that it is not true that all things are advantageous. "All things are under my power," as you say, but one should add that, " I will not let myself be brought under the power of anything." The Corinthians had boldly stated in their letter and had turned to their own use—of course with a view to full Christian freedom—the philosophic doctrine that "man is the measure of all things," that the individual is master of his surroundings and of his fate. Turned to a Christian application, this doctrine naturally suited their exuberant satisfaction with themselves and with their steady development and improvement. Along with it they had used the other expression quoted by Paul in 8:1: "We know that we all have knowledge," to which he so often alludes throughout the epistle.[2]

Paul saw clearly the dangerous extremes to which this doctrine was liable to be pushed; and the fact that he quotes it at this point suggests that he believed it to have been used, or to be likely to be used, by his correspondents in the way indicated and combated in 6:13ff. In fact, it is natural to suppose that the words, "meats for the belly, and the belly for meats," are quoted from the mouth of the Corinthians; and the argument is turned aside by Paul thus: "You say that each part of the body has its natural function, and is rightly directed to the performance thereof, but you forget the distinction between what is perishable, and what is permanent in the body." If that be true, then the Corinthians must have mentioned that naturalistic theory, either urging it as true or professing their inability to refute its logical consequences.

The commentators quote various passages from ancient writers to show that Corinth was a specially vicious city. It may be doubted, however, whether there was much difference between the tone there and in the Aegean world generally. The serious danger lay, not in any excess of vice there[3]—for excess tends rather to produce a reaction in the opposite direction—but in the low moral standard that was practically universal in society. Paul is not arguing against the criminality of a Nero, but against the naturalistic theories of educated, thinking, and comparatively well-living men.

21

Marriage

Chapter 7 is difficult and, to the historical student, disappointing. It is disappointing because, though it treats of marriage—a subject peculiarly well adapted to throw light on the state of society in Corinth—yet the treatment is so general as to give little information about the Corinthians in particular. It is difficult because Paul is here answering a question which had been addressed to him by the church in Corinth, and his reply and arguments are evidently influenced much by the terms in which the question was stated and the ideas on the subject revealed thereby among the Corinthians. Yet the reply gives no very clear evidence as to the terms and tone of the question.

There are not many passages in Paul's writings that have given rise to so many divergent and incorrect views as this chapter. Some of those views relate to the practical conclusions to be drawn from the chapter, as, for example, that celibacy and monasticism were recommended by the apostle as the ideal system of life for those who are strong enough morally. Others relate to his own situation in life. Was he a widower, or had he ever been married? In the course of the chapter he several times mentions his own example and his own condition; and it is still a matter of keen debate whether his words imply that he had been married or not. Now if Paul had been discussing the question whether it is better to marry or remain single, it is hardly conceivable, in view of his direct, uncompromising, and emphatic way of stating his opinions, that he should, in quoting his own example, speak so vaguely as to leave such an issue uncertain. He would either make no reference to his own example, or he would so speak of it as to leave it clear on which side his example told (see chapter 22).

But it is clear that the question which was in his mind was not whether marriage or celibacy is the better way of life, and that he does not quote his own case as an example and pattern whether one should marry. When he mentions himself here, he is not thinking of that, and therefore his words do not permit any sure inference on the point. To treat this chapter as if the question under discussion were the comparative advantages of marriage and celibacy is to approach it from the wrong point of view, and misinterpretation is unavoidable.

Moreover, on that commonly accepted view, the whole passage in 7:1ff. suggests a conception of the nature and purpose of marriage that is very far from lofty or noble, as if marriage were a mere concession to the weakness of human nature, to save mankind from worse evil. But such a conception is irreconcilable with Paul's language elsewhere: such was not his attitude toward marriage. As we have seen in the preceding section, marriage was in his estimation the type of the union between Christ and the church, and therefore on the highest plane of ideal excellence and purity.

Now, as we have seen in chapters 13 and 19, we must be disposed to suspect quotation or allusion to views and arguments of the Corinthians, when we find in this epistle statements that stand in marked contrast with Paul's known opinions elsewhere. He expressly mentions in 7:1 that he is taking up a topic at the point where the Corinthians had left it; and his words would be so understood by them. We must try to take the subject up at the same point; but it is not easy to restore the words of the lost letter.

The crucial point in the whole passage is the opening statement: "It is good for man not to come into connection with woman.[1] Evidently this is said in relation to a Corinthian statement or question. In rightly catching the nature of that statement or question lies the key to the interpretation of the crucial point.

Comparison of two other passages will throw some light on this statement, alike through the resemblances and through the differences.

(1). 7:38 reads: "So then both he who gives his own virgin daughter in marriage does well; and he who does not give her in marriage shall do better.[2]

Here is a distinct, positive statement, followed by a comparison between two courses of action: one is good, but another is better. But to express the comparison a comparative degree is necessary. Now in 7:1 there is only the positive degree, καλόν; and we must infer that the meaning is not (as many readers assume), "it is better for man not to marry, but by a concession to weakness marriage is permitted." Such a meaning would require the use of the comparative degree. In fact the analogy of 7:38 would rather suggest that 7:1 implies "it is good to avoid marriage, but better to marry."

We observe also that a wrong meaning is often drawn from 7:38. Paul does not there say, "it is good for a virgin to marry, but better for her not to marry." What he says is very different: "It is good for a father to seek out a husband for his daughter, but better not to seek out a husband for her. There is no reason why the father should regard it as his bounden duty to give her a husband: he is quite justified if he leaves her in her unmarried state. It is good, it is not wrong, for a woman to be unmarried."

Must we not see here a gentle plea for individual right of judgment? Paul would not interfere with the established rule of society, that it is the parent's place to seek a husband for the daughter; but he adds the proviso that there is no inexorable duty placed on the parent to find a husband for her: it is even better if the father puts no compulsion on his daughter.

(2) 7:39–40 reads: "If the husband be dead, the wife is free to be married to whom she will; only in the Lord. But she is happier if she abide as she is, after my judgment."[3]

Here again we observe that when the two states, second marriage and avoidance thereof, are compared, the comparative degree is used. Also, the avoidance of second marriage is declared to be not better but happier. Paul's own judgment—which he believes to be influenced by divine inspiration (7:40)—tells him that such is more likely to lead to true happiness. But he will place on the widow no shadow of compulsion in the way of duty.

From these cases the inference is clear. In 7:1ff. Paul lays down the principle: "It is good, it is permissible, it is not wrong, for people to remain unmarried provided absolute purity is observed." That condition, however, was so difficult in Greek society that the apostle is obliged to go on, verse after verse, urging the immense advantage of married life from that point of view, but not at all implying that the essential feature of marriage lies therein.

The point of view, then, which Paul assumes in 7:1 is that marriage is not an absolute duty, but is relative to the individual nature and character. Each individual man or woman must judge for himself or herself whether it conduces to the perfecting of their life to marry. There is no moral principle constraining them to marriage; on the contrary, it is a fine thing, an excellent thing, to remain unmarried (7:1–8).

That point of view seems to imply that the Corinthians had put the question whether the view widely entertained alike among Jews and pagans—that everyone ought to marry in the ordinary course of life at the proper age—was correct. Paul strongly discountenances that view: marriage is not an obligation imposed by society and by nature on all persons. The individual is here master of his fate, and ought to judge for himself, and be answerable only to his own conscience. We see here a claim for the emancipation of the individual judgment from the bonds that society had imposed on it. Freedom is Paul's ideal; but he dare not use the word so much to the Greeks—always predisposed to lawlessness, to the overexaltation of the rights of the individual, and to over-assertion of the principle that "all things are lawful unto me"—as he could to the submissive and slavish Phrygians.[4]

It is not improbable that the Corinthians actually quoted the public law, as it existed under the Roman Empire. It is at least highly probable, and indeed practically inevitable, that they were thinking of that legal duty. The legislation of Augustus had been directed to encourage marriage. By a succession of laws,[5] that emperor had endeavored to make marriage universal, had imposed penalties of growing severity on the unmarried, and had bestowed honors and privileges on the parents of a family. The emperor's aim was, undoubtedly, lofty and noble: he sought to check the modern tendency to immorality and profligacy, and to restore the old Roman purity and simplicity of family life. Society approved in theory his principle, which in practice it disregarded. His method was that of compulsion.[6]

So also the Jewish practice not merely urged marriage as a universal duty, but attached honors and privileges to marriage; for example, one could not be a member of the Sanhedrin unless one were both married and a parent.

The theory of the empire was that the emperor was the father and director and counselor of all his subjects. The emperor told them what to do, and it was their part to pay implicit obedience to all his orders. Against that theory Christianity protested: it claimed the right of individual judgment. Paul fully sympathized with the aim of Augustus, and he also entirely recognized that family life is the most effective check to immorality (7:2–9). But, as in all his teaching, so here he advocates freedom. All should judge for themselves, and undertake voluntarily the duties of marriage only after full consideration, if they think it best. No compulsion should be put on them, either by giving superior honors to the married, or by putting discredit on the unmarried. The only discredit lay in profligacy: it is quite honorable to be unmarried, if one lives a pure life.

If we have rightly apprehended the character of the question addressed to Paul by the Corinthians, then it follows that the common view is erroneous. It is commonly said that the section of the church in Corinth which "was of Cephas" upheld marriage because Cephas was married, while the section which "was of Paul" argued that single life was better because Paul was either unmarried or a widower; and their dispute was referred to the apostle for decision. We have already seen that much of the theorizing as to the doctrines held by the four supposed parties in Corinth proceeds on a wrong interpretation of Paul's words; and that the parties were not nearly so definitely opposed to one another as those theories assume. Now we find that the question propounded to Paul by the Corinthians was not "is it better to marry or not?" but rather "is it to be regarded as a duty incumbent on Christians to marry, as the Jews and the Roman law maintain?"

22

The Corinthian View Regarding Marriage

In the preceding section we take the view that the Corinthians had proposed to Paul the question whether the right principle of life was that all persons ought to marry. We must now ask what was their intention in putting this question.

The answer has already been distinctly indicated in the reasoning which led up to the determination of the question which they proposed to the apostle. The letter of the Corinthians was (as we have seen already at various points) a decidedly ambitious performance. They discussed, with much philosophic acumen and with strong reforming zeal, the nature of society, the character of man, the relation of man to God, and other similar topics; and they were well satisfied with the letter which embodied their opinions. It was (as they felt) able, religious, and on a lofty plane of morality. They were eager to regenerate and reform society, and they were satisfied that they knew how to do so. The questions which they put to Paul on this subject were calculated to show clearly what answer must, in their opinion, be given to them.

In no part of the Roman Empire was there current at that time any idea of the advisability and the superior purity of monasticism and the permanent separation of the sexes. The Corinthians were entirely under the influence of prevailing views, and were as firmly persuaded as all the leading official moralists were, that the admitted and palpable degeneracy of society was connected with the unwillingness to marry, which was spreading widely among the most fashionable and corrupt section of society in the empire. The most vicious part of society was the one where celibacy was commonest. The classes which were purest in life—the Jews and, at a long interval behind them, the old-fashioned pagans—were those among which marriage was almost universal. They drew the obvious conclusion: make marriage universal, and vice will disappear.

That such was the drift of the Corinthians' argument is clear from Paul's reply. He fully admits (7:2–5) the truth that lies in their reasoning, and is involved in human nature. Among other things they had evidently referred to the preference for childlessness, which was characteristic of fashionable society under the empire, and Paul quite agreed with their views on this point. Marriage should be a real union. A married couple ought to live together regularly. They may, by mutual consent, live separate occasionally for a time, with a view to religious and devotional purposes. Such temporary separation was a recognized custom in society, and Paul saw no reason to interfere with it, but rather inclines to commend it. Still he safeguards himself by adding (7:6) that he only allows, but does not enjoin, such periodic temporary separation.[1]

But this view of marriage as a safeguard from evil is not a high one: it is not Paul's. "I would," he says in 7:7, "that all men were even as I myself;" and that they needed no such safeguard, but could live on a higher plane and look on marriage from a nobler point of view. But such is not the case, and men must guide their life according to their own nature. They have "each his own gift from God," each his own special weakness and special strength. Paul never legislates as if all were like each other or like himself. All must judge according to their own nature and conscience—in the spirit of God.

In 7:10ff. the subject is taken up afresh from a different side; but, as we shall see in a following section, the tone of advice is the same. Every man is quite justified in remaining in his present condition, unmarried or married; in other words, the suggestion, which was evidently made by the Corinthians, that the unmarried should be urged to marry, was strongly repudiated by Paul

It was the insistence of the Corinthians on that lower view of marriage that led Paul to devote some attention to it. They were not able to rise above current philosophy and popular morality. Their zeal to reform society opened up to them no lofty or mystic views, but kept them on a strictly utilitarian level. Marriage was a useful thing for the purpose on which they were bent, and was deserving of every encouragement. Ardent reformers usually have a *nostrum*, and the Corinthians had their complete cure for the ills of society. They were ready and eager to take the laws of nature under their own special care, and see that they were carried out. Many people have shown the same zeal to protect nature and her laws since the Corinthians wrote.

But, indubitably, the prominence which—in his desire to acknowledge fully the proportion of truth in their letter—Paul gives to the lower view of marriage, led to much misapprehension. Misapprehension was exaggerated, not long after his time, by another cause. The revolt from the impurity of common society led to an exaggeration of the spiritual value of mere physical purity of life, however attained. The distorted views of life which spread widely in Christian circles inevitably produced complete misconception of Paul's views. His language to the Corinthians lent itself readily to misinterpretation, and the age was not one which would wait to compare passage with passage and weigh each, in order to form a reasoned theory of Paul's views as a whole. Many sentences in this chapter, taken by themselves, could easily be read as inculcating that marriage is an evil, permissible only because it saves the world from still greater evils; and they have been so read.

But to suppose that the Corinthians could have been thinking of the problems of monasticism, and could have questioned Paul as to whether the virtues of celibacy were not such as to render it a specially laudable and meritorious course, is quite anachronistic. People on their plane of thought and knowledge could not have entertained such thoughts.

23

Was Paul Married?

We have seen that, on the commonly accepted view as to the question which is here discussed by Paul, it is not possible to find any distinct evidence as to Paul's own condition. God and trustworthy authorities read different meanings in the passage. But, as we have now determined the form of the Corinthians' question, the case is changed. It appears hardly probable that, if Paul had never had a wife, the Corinthians would have put to him the question, "Is it to be regarded as a duty incumbent on all Christians to marry?" Had he been unmarried always, the question answered itself.

But it must be acknowledged that this argument is subjective, and depends much for its value on individual feeling. There is little real argument on the point to be deduced from Paul's own words here or elsewhere. He often urges his own example on his converts, but never in reference to such a matter as this. He urges on them to live a life as entirely devoted to the divine purpose as himself. He was absolutely certain that the divine will had wholly occupied his mind and powers, and he wishes that others were like him in that respect. But he never could hold, he never held, his own action to be a pattern to others in such matters as marriage. He never would have said, "Marry as I have married," or "remain unmarried like me."

To my individual judgment it appears that Paul's mind shows a peculiar power of universal sympathy, which is more characteristic of a man who had been married. But, on the other hand, who can venture to set any limit to his marvelous power of comprehending the mind and feelings of his converts?

The question of Paul's marriage or celibacy has considerable importance for the interpretation of the chapter which we are now studying. Evidence on the question has usually been sought from

7:7–8. This, however, seems to misconceive the force of those verses. When Paul wishes (7:7) "that all men were even as I myself," he is not thinking of his condition as regards marriage, but of his nature and character. His words carried more meaning, doubtless, to those who knew him personally than they do to us. Those who had been acquainted with him knew how impossible to him an impure wife was, how inevitable purity was to him. But even to us the words are full of meaning, as is set forth in chapter 25 on "Marriage and the Divine Life."

When one looks at the case dispassionately, it seems altogether inconsistent with the context that Paul, who is here emphasizing the injudiciousness of laying down any universal law and the necessity of conceding much to the individual varieties of situation, should express the wish either that all men were married and widowers, or that all men were unmarried.[1] It is reasonable and natural that he should wish that all men were of such character that a perfectly pure life was as easy to them as to himself; but it is altogether absurd that he should say, "I would that all men were widowers," or "that all were celibate." The first of these two alternatives is so supremely absurd that we may almost sympathize with those many interpreters who have recoiled from it and have championed the less absurd alternative "that all should be celibate." The latter has been the more dangerous interpretation, because it is less palpably absurd. But no one who has any real sympathy with Paul's spirit can imagine him expressing, even in the most abstract fashion, the wish that there could or should be one universal rule—no marriage, no union between man and woman in the world.

The expression in 7:8 is not to be taken as a new subject and a new paragraph; it is only a summing up of 7:1–7, as we shall see in the following section. The rendering of the Authorized Version brings that out clearly. The Revised Version takes a view, and emphasizes it by an arrangement of the paragraphs, which we must think false. It is peculiarly unfortunate that in a Revised Version there should be so many cases in which we must recur to the older version, even while we acknowledge that in the overwhelming majority of cases the changes made in the Revised Version are either needed, or at least not wrong. But it must be granted that paragraph arrangement is often inadequate to express the closely welded thought of Paul's epistles.

24

Remarriage

The question of "the unmarried and widows" comes up in 7:8. Who are "the unmarried?" (ἀγάμοις), and why are they thus mixed up with the question of remarriage?

There is no question that in classical Greek ἄγαμος meant "one who has never been married," and ἀγαμία "celibacy." It would not be easy to find any justification for taking ἄγαμος in the sense of one who, after being married, has lost his wife. Yet that sense has been championed in this passage by many commentators, who have been misled by the desire to make ἀγάμοις the masculine corresponding to χήραις, the feminine. Some of these champions of a false Greek even allege that there was no Greek word for "widower," and therefore that Paul had to press the word ἄγαμος wrongly into his service for the occasion. But Paul knew Greek better than those commentators, who had not troubled to consult the lexicons before they asserted a negative.

Paul used χήραις preferably to χήροις—though generally a masculine term is used when both sexes are to be included—because the feminine is much the more characteristic idea in this case, just as English "widow" is the simple and "widower" the derivative (contrary to the usual practice in such pairs of term). He here sums up "those who have never known marriage (ἀγάμοις) and those who have been married and widowed." In 7:8 the apostle sums up and repeats the advice of 7:1–7: to remain without a consort is a respectable, honorable course of life, if they remain pure in that situation "like me."[1] Otherwise marriage is their only way of living rightly.

Moreover, in 7:39–40 it is clear that Paul thought the question of marriage was not altogether the same for a widow and a widower. A widow occupied, in his view, a distinct and peculiar position as regards remarriage, and he is much more decisive in his advice to widows than to any other class of persons. As we have already seen in chapter 21, his opinion was that, though a widow was perfectly free and right in marrying again, yet she was "happier" to remain in her widowhood (7:40). That is the only case throughout this much misunderstood chapter in which he expresses a distinct opinion against marriage.

But as to widowers, Paul evidently thought that the question to them was not essentially different from the question in the case of unmarried men. The widow occupied a special and peculiar position; not so the widower. There was therefore no special advice needed for him.

Thus, from every point of view, we see that Paul in 7:8 sums up his advice as affecting (1) all as yet unmarried persons; (2) widows. There was no third class requiring special treatment. If in any small degree widowers differed from the first class, they may be taken under the second class.

The opinions stated in this chapter, so far as we have yet seen them, must be pronounced eminently sensible and practical and suitable. But, at the same time, there is an evident want of the loftier tone that is characteristic of Paul's mind. We have seen that the prominence of the plain but rather commonplace tone is due to the necessity under which Paul was placed of considering the Corinthians' questions from their own point of view. But we must proceed to ask how far his conception of the Christian life as the divine life was permitted to appear, even in addressing the Corinthian "wise" men, a not wholly sympathetic audience.

25

Marriage and the Divine Life

In writing to a community of recent converts from heathenism, St. Paul's expression was necessarily controlled and guided throughout by the consideration of what should be most easily intelligible to them. He was not composing a formal religious or philosophical treatise, where the writer might aim at an ideally complete and philosophically clear exposition. He was writing about immediate practical needs to persons whose views and power of understanding were strongly affected by their past experience as pagans, and it was useless to write except as they could understand.

Paul would never have been the great teacher of the Gentiles unless he had been in complete sympathy with them, unless he had been perfectly conscious of their needs and how to meet them, unless he had been perfectly able to drive home his ideas into their minds. That does not imply that he could make all the thoughts and sentiments and truths of this epistle perfectly intelligible to all the Corinthians. On the contrary, there were in all his epistles many things that none of his readers would understand at the moment, some that they would probably never come to understand fully. There were probably even things that he himself did not fully understand in all their bearings as he wrote them,[1] things truer than even he knew, things which he saw dimly with the prophet's eye and could not measure precisely with the philosopher's intelligence.

But still, Paul always had his audience clear before him. He was writing in each case a letter to a definite group of persons in a definite situation, and he wrote with a view to their powers of comprehending what he said. We cannot doubt that he often chose a mode of expression because it was specially suited to the comprehension of this particular group of persons, and that he would have selected a different expression to a group in another quarter of the world.[2] We should therefore never lose sight of the audience which he had in mind. We should always ask what meaning they would be likely to take from the words used; and if we can satisfy ourselves that they would naturally have taken the words of Paul in a certain way, we may be confident that Paul must have foreseen their understanding. It does not follow, of course, that the meaning which they would naturally take from his words was all that lay in them; but at least it was within Paul's consciousness as he wrote.

That men and women should devote themselves, at least occasionally for a short time, to the "divine life," separating themselves from the ordinary life of society during that period, was a common practice in the ancient world. That some should devote themselves permanently to that life in the divine service was also an accepted fact in all the more enthusiastic and deep kinds of religion. The prophets among the Hebrews, and "they that abode forever before the LORD" (1 Sam. 1:22, 28), had their analogues in the pagan cults. But religions differed widely in their conception of the sphere and character of the "divine life." In some of the pagan forms of religion the "divine life" was one which, from our point of view, was lower morally even than the low standard of ordinary pagan society,[3] and yet it was often from real religious devotion that people consecrated themselves, temporarily or permanently, to such life.

The Corinthian converts, therefore, were quite conversant with the idea that individuals might temporarily or permanently arrange their life, not according to the common rules and practices incumbent on the majority of human beings in society, but according to a special rule of service to the divine will. They would easily and naturally take the further step, and realize that the rules of Christian service would be very different from those which they had known in their pagan days. They would then desire to understand what were the Christian rules of service.

But, on the other hand, the people of Corinth were not an Oriental race with an almost infinite capacity and yearning for the more enthusiastic and self-forgetting forms of religious sentiment. They were partly dominated by the practical, hard, matter-of-fact Roman spirit; but still more they were Greek in character, with a natural temperament which loved clear scientific definition and gracefully ordered expression in action and in language,[4] which was so unfavorable to anything like extravagance or enthusiasm or disorderliness in religion as to be fatal even to vitality and reality in it. I do not mean that the Greeks were as a race nonreligious. No race is. Time after time in Greek history the craving of human nature for religion favored the introduction of Oriental forms of worship. But in every case the Greek character gradually toned down the

Oriental fervor and self-forgettingness of the new cult, smoothed away its excesses, lightened its spirit, imparted order, regularity, harmony, artistic character to its natural free exuberance, and ended by depriving it of vital power, so that the same process of introduction, assimilation, and destruction was soon free to begin in respect of another fresh Oriental cult.

The pressure exercised on St. Paul by the character of the people whom he was addressing is specially strongly marked in the chapter in which he replies to their questions about marriage. He is, of course, only answering questions, not propounding a general view as to the nature of the marriage relation and its place in religion and life; and what he has to say is to some extent limited by that fact. But still there is observable often in chapter 7 a pragmatical and commonplace character, a restriction of the view to mere details, a want of life and warmth, and a poverty and dryness, which can be explained in a letter of Paul's only by the necessity of adapting his explanations to the power of understanding in his audience.

In the chapter now before us it is apparent that the "divine life" is much in Paul's mind, and that in many sentences he is thinking of the relation of marriage to the divine life. Is marriage consistent with the divine life, or favorable to it? The general impression which the chapter would convey to the Corinthians, undoubtedly, was that Christians who aimed at living the "divine life" might try whether they were able to rise above the need of marriage, and that those who devoted themselves for only a brief season to the "divine life" might separate themselves for the time from their consorts, with their consent, in order to concentrate their undivided attention on the "things of God." But these are the exceptions which Paul makes to the general rule of marriage, which the Corinthians have been advocating, and which he tacitly accepts—with these exceptions. As in various other cases, the fact which fills the mind of both writer and reader is not expressly mentioned, just because it is so strongly present to his readers (see chapter 27).

But what is the "divine life?" It is obvious that Paul vibrates between two conceptions of the "divine life."

1. In the mystic view, in which Paul commonly lived and moved and wrote, every Christian must be living the "divine life," for he becomes a Christian only when Christ lives in him. The life of faith is the life of Christ, the "divine life"; and all true Christians, whatever be their outward position in the world, are equally living that life. In this more mystical view the marriage tie between two Christians is not inconsistent with the "divine life," for it is compared by St. Paul to the relation between Christ and the church.[5] So

far from either party to the marriage tie being a hindrance to the other in the "divine life," each is a help to the other. Each, living for the other, is raised out of self, as the church lives in Christ and Christ in the church.

Such is the spirit in Paul's letter to the Asian churches (Eph. 5:22–23). Such too seems to be the thought in his mind in the enigmatic words in a later part of the present epistle (11:11): "Howbeit neither is the woman without the man, nor the man without the woman, in the Lord." In the previous verses the apostle has been showing that man and woman are not two exactly similar and equal things: man is the primary and woman the complementary, created to complete and perfect the primary, meaningless and purposeless without the primary. But he adds in verse 11, the primary—man—also is equally imperfect without the complementary—woman—"in the Lord," that is, in the "divine life."[6] The "divine life" lies in the perfect realization of the nature of these complementary things through the mutual tie that binds them. If our view be right, then that sentence (11:11) may be paraphrased thus: "While woman is dependent on man, man equally is incomplete apart from woman, when they are regarded on the plane of the divine life."

To understand chapter 7 properly in its relation to Paul's thought, we must take it along with chapter 9, or rather, we must take it in connection with the living thought of the whole epistle. It is characteristic of Paul's torrent-like pouring forth of his mind in a letter[7] that frequently in the present epistle he does not exhaust, by a formal exposition, what he has to say on one topic before he passes to the next. The reader must go on to the end before he can fully gather Paul's mind on any of the questions that were put to him. To him they are all parts of one whole. Each one works into the other; and he passes from one to the other as they touch one another. Thus, in 10:16–22 he begins to speak of the communion of the Christian with Christ, and his exposition rises to a higher plane. He becomes more immediately and presently conscious of the "divine life." He feels that some of the topics which he has already touched on require to be raised to this loftier plane in order that their full significance may be set before the Corinthians. In 10:23–33 he resumes the topic of chapter 8, and in 11:3–16 he resumes the topic of chapter 7. He shows how the mystic idea of the "divine life" must be taken into account before either topic can be properly seen. Then he takes up again and completes the subject begun in 10:16–22.

2. In chapter 7 the thought of the "divine life" is present in a more commonplace, nonmystic form. The immediate practical

fact—which doubtless was involved in some of the questions addressed to him by the Corinthians—was that the life and occupations of the various members of a Christian congregation varied much, and that some had their minds more fully occupied with the actual ordinary business of life, while others turned their attention more to the work of the church. It is clear from other passages in the epistle that this diversity of duties caused a good deal of care and hesitation to the Corinthians, and filled some space in their letter. There was considerable competition in church service, and some argument as to the comparative importance and honor of the various duties (12:4ff.). Already at this early stage the broad distinction was becoming clear in Corinth between ordinary business and church work—of course not, as yet, between clergy and laity (which distinction was much later in growing up), but rather between work for the common good and work for private interest. The distinction arose naturally among Greek or Roman citizens: it was the obvious and inevitable development of their previous ideas about the way of conducting societies and municipalities. The Corinthians, in putting their questions and suggestions to Paul, took the natural view that the work for the common good was among the "things of the Lord"—in short, was a branch of the "divine life," while work for private interest was restricted to the "things of the world."

In the seventh chapter Paul moves on this lower plane of thought, as his readers required: he treats their questions on the same level on which they were conceived. Consequently the whole impresses the reader as lacking distinction and finality and philosophic clarity , and as rather shrewdly practical and containing much good plain common sense. "He that is unmarried is careful for the things of the Lord, how he may please the Lord: but he that is married is careful for the things of the world, how he may please his wife" (v. 33). A saying like that is undeniable—on one side and in a certain considerable degree—but it is insufficient, it is disappointing, it touches sharply the weakness of human nature, and it touches nothing more—one might almost say it approximates to the level of Lord Chesterfield's *Letters to His Son*.

Yet in the struggling life of the young community of Corinth, it was unavoidable that these questions should emerge and should demand treatment in this practical, commonsense spirit. This chapter is a remarkable proof of the many-sidedness of St. Paul's nature, of his capacity for guiding his young churches in every part of their life, of his intense practicality where the practical mind was needed. At the same time it is a remarkable proof of the danger of taking any passage of the epistles by itself as a complete exposition instead of judging it in relation to the circumstances of the audience to which it was addressed. How misleading a conception we should gather of St. Paul's ideas on this subject, if we could not turn to other passages and compare them with this chapter!

It follows necessarily from the nature of Paul's letters that they insist most on what is lacking in his readers, that the writer tries to build up his readers, to complete their character, to lay stress on whatever is weakest in them. To the servile spirit of the Phrygians Paul emphasizes the importance of freedom; to the self-assertive and unruly spirit of the Greeks he emphasizes the need of obedience to laws and institutions and general principles of conduct;[8] to the Corinthians, who had suggested that compulsory marriage might be a useful thing in the church, and "gravely doubted whether a fixed condition of celibacy was right in itself and according to God's will for man,"[9] he insisted on the inexpedience of enforcing marriage on all, and on the advantages that celibacy might offer, amid the practical difficulties of their situation in Corinth, to a certain limited number of persons. The Corinthians had referred to "the perils and suspicions[10] to which the unwedded were exposed" in Corinth. Paul replied that "in view of the straitness now imminent," the principle is justifiable "to be as one is" (v. 26)—an enigmatic expression in the Greek—for the time is shortened, and the day will soon come when all temporary distinctions shall be obliterated, when "the fashion of this world is passing away" (v. 31). It is remarkable that here marriage is ranked along with the merely ephemeral differences, such as comfort or misery, wealth or poverty. But wherever marriage is discouraged it is regarded on that lower level; where Paul thinks of man in his relation to God, free from the shackles of sin, he sees marriage in the loftier aspect.

But while we find the other side of Paul's thought in passages like 1 Corinthians 11:11 and Ephesians 5:23ff., in the Pastoral Epistles we find much the same side as here in 1 Corinthians 7. There, as here, Paul is concerned with the practical needs of young and growing communities of Christians amid the society of Greco-Roman towns. It happens to be forced on him there to insist more on the positive side, and to urge the importance of marriage. The danger which he foresaw was "that in later times some shall fall away from the faith . . . forbidding to marry, and commanding to abstain from meats" (1 Tim. 4:1, 3). It was, therefore, just as necessary for his purpose to emphasize the practical value of marriage in Christian society, as it is here to point out that individuals should be free to follow the bent of their own nature, if it leads them to avoid marriage and devote themselves to the "things of God." There men and women are, on the whole, advised to marry once. Those who are to devote themselves to work in the congregation and among the poor as widows, deacons, or bishops will be all the better fitted for it by the experience of marriage, but are to avoid a second marriage. Hence the repeated and much discussed rule that all those class officials as to be "the wife of one man" or "the husband of one wife." But no reference is made to such officials as apostles, prophets, etc., who were not chosen by the church, but marked out by the divine will. Paul has them much in mind when he pleads to the Corinthians for the right of celibacy: his view is that, if God has put celibacy in their mind and nature, they should not be urged by church rules (such as the Corinthians proposed) to marry. But when he wrote to Timothy or Titus about the practical work of governing a church, it was unnecessary to speak of those personages who lay outside the range of ordinary government.

We see thus the essential identity of the teaching on this subject of St. Paul in all his epistles, in spite of apparent differences, due to his emphasizing most the part that was most needed for his immediate purpose. In one respect only is there any development or change, and that is in the principle that those who are to engage in the practical or administrative work of the congregation, male or female, as bishops (i.e., presbyters), deacons, or "widows," ought to be married, but should not be a second time married. But while this does differ from the views expressed in 1 Corinthians 7, the development is an easy one. The experience of married life is regarded as an aid in the practical working of Christian society. But there is nothing to show that Paul ever came to regard it as an aid to the prophet or the teacher or the speaker with tongues in the congregation. On the contrary, there is every appearance that in those callings, which may more truly be described as the "divine life," the teaching of 1 Corinthians 7 continued until the end of his life.

In 7:17 Paul asserts the identity of his teaching in all his churches. The assertion applies, in the first place, only to the principle that everyone should accept the lot in which he is placed—the principle which he could never utter too strongly. Here he devotes verses 17–24 to a very full and emphatic statement of it. But in a secondary sense, it applies to his whole teaching. Rightly understood, it was the same everywhere. Acts 14:23 and 16:4 are to be applied to all his later churches.

26

Apologia Pro Vita Sua

Before passing from this subject I may refer again to one point in regard to which further thought has changed my view. The view was stated above in chapter 23 that, while very little of the supposed evidence really bore on the point, the Corinthians would hardly have ventured to suggest to Paul that all Christians should marry, if he himself had never been married. This view seems to me now to be a mistake, and this chapter appears hardly quite fully intelligible except on the supposition that Paul had never been married. If I now alter the view formerly expressed with hesitation, it is evident that at least I had no prejudice in favor of the view which is now stated here.

It is not that I think the interpretation of 7:7 which is given on page 71 is incorrect or doubtful. It still seems necessary. Also, the interpretation of 7:8 as referring to "unmarried" persons in general (not restricted to "widowers," as many think) still appears to me to furnish no argument bearing on this question. It is true that the advice given them to "abide even as I" cannot be taken as exactly parallel to "were even as I myself" in the previous verse. In 7:7 St. Paul speaks of permanent personal nature and character; but in verse 8 the word "abide" shows this to be impossible. When the unmarried are advised to "abide even as I," the alternative is clearly implied that they might, if they chose, cease to abide so and change their condition. Hence the idea in Paul's mind is a changeable fact, not a permanent and unalterable quality of nature. The meaning must therefore be, "I say to the unmarried and to widows, it is a way of life worthy of all respect to remain without a spouse (as I myself do)." But that affords no distinct criterion for deciding the question: Paul could equally well say that whether he were celibate or widower.

The decisive consideration seems to be in two arguments. The first is founded on 9:5, where Paul claims that he has as full a right to be accompanied by a wife when he goes round his churches as the rest of the apostles. If he had been a widower, his words would imply that he is maintaining his right to marry a second wife, but it seems more in keeping with his character that, in that case, he should have given a different form to his retort. It is a reasonable retort to say, "I have every right to marry, and take about a wife with me, like the other apostles," while the readers know from chapter 7 what were his reasons for remaining unmarried. But it seems a somewhat tasteless and unsuitable retort, if his wife was dead, to say, "I have every right to marry a second wife." But if this be too subjective or hypercritical, the next argument seems much stronger.

The second consideration lies in the relation of chapter 9 to the preceding. The strength with which Paul there asserts his rights as against the other apostles seems hardly explicable, unless it were called forth by something in the Corinthians' letter which he felt to be a slight. The reference to his own example in 8:13 leads on naturally to the assertion of his right to be a model to them; but it does not explain the tone of the assertion, which is distinctly that of defense against attack or disrespect. Now there is not the slightest appearance either in chapter 8 or in 10:23–33 that the remarks or questions of the Corinthians about meats contained anything which could be so construed. Paul answers in such a way as to show that their questions were sensible, well-conceived, and practical; while his reply is entirely in the line of explanation and defense of the teaching of the apostles generally on the subject (see chapter 28), not of difference from them in any respect. Yet he goes off immediately afterwards into a vindication of his rights over against the other apostles. That becomes explicable only when we bear in mind that in their questions about marriage the Corinthians, tacitly or explicitly, had contrasted St. Paul's conduct with that of the other apostles, and had indicated their view that the other apostles had taken the course which Christians ought to follow. Chapter 9 verse 1 resumes the topic of chapter 7.

Now, though to our modern ways of thinking, such a difference of opinion may seem too unimportant to rouse any feeling on either side, yet if we judge by what is the best modern representative of the old Jewish opinion on the subject, namely, Muslim and especially Arab opinion, we shall find that Paul must always have been sensitive on this subject. Lane[1] mentions that his neighbors in one quarter of Cairo would not permit him to live there because he had no wife with him; and that in another quarter, where the people were less strict, they were constantly urging him to make himself respectable by marrying; and the advice was not jocular, but given in all seriousness. Israel Abrahams speaks very strongly of Jewish ideas on this subject (though his words refer to a later time, yet they are not untrue of earlier times): the rabbi was expected and even compelled to marry, and hence his "home became at once the center of a bright, cultured circle, and the model which other homes imitated."[2]

So strong must this compelling force have been in St. Paul's time that some modern scholars have even maintained that he must necessarily have been married. That is not justifiable, however, for his point of view was not wholly unknown in Jewish circles. As my friend, Professor William P. Paterson, pointed out to me, "Rabbi Asai took no wife: my soul, said he, cleaves to the Law, let others see to the upbuilding of the world."[3]

Moreover, it is evident that Paul was often accused by his Jewish opponents of being a Sadducee, or no better than a Sadducee. Hence, when he was brought before the Sanhedrin in Jerusalem, his first words were directed to disprove that charge. "I am a Pharisee, and the son of a Pharisee" (Acts 23:3; cf. Phil. 3:6). Now celibacy was a Roman practice, and the unmarried Jew exposed himself to the charge of imitating Roman manners like a Sadducee.[4] In that age the charge was annoying and even serious.

In the circumstances one can understand why Paul was touched on a sore point by the Corinthian question, whether it would not be advisable that all Christians should be married like the apostles and the Jews generally. Incidentally it may be added that one desiderates in Professor Findlay's reconstruction of that part of the Corinthian letter to St. Paul some clearer expression contrasting him with the other apostles.

If Paul chose celibacy, he must have done so while still a Jew, and there can hardly be any doubt that he chose from similar motives to Rabbi Asai. Much of chapter 7 reads like an expansion and wider application of the Rabbi's principle, especially verses 29–34, where the obvious meaning is that marriage prevents the concentration of one's whole powers on the "divine life" and the things of the Lord. St. Paul, like Rabbi Asai, had resolved, even before he became a Christian, to devote himself to the work of God; and his conversion merely changed the direction of his activity and his conception of God's demands, but was not the first cause of his devotion. He believed, while he was persecuting the Christians, that he was as entirely concentrated on God's work as afterwards when he had become a Christian.

And now in writing to the Corinthians, he makes in chapter 7 his defense of his original choice. His defense throws a new light on his pre-Christian life, showing him "cleaving to the Law" and renouncing the ordinary life of society for his own conception of the "divine life." This is a subject on which much remains to be said, but which is out of place here.

27

The Corinthian Philosophers

The questions put by the Corinthians to St. Paul were suggested to them by the pressing calls and difficulties of their present situation—a scanty, needy group, almost submerged in the surrounding ocean of paganism, keeping their heads above it only with difficulty, and with a constant tendency to sink again beneath the surface.

The Christians in Corinth had just risen out of the dead level of paganism. The first effort had carried them clear above the surface; but reaction was inevitable, and with it many of them were in danger of sinking back again—probably some actually did sink.

We all know how difficult it is to sustain one's self permanently above the moral level of society, and with what force surrounding society continually presses us into itself. But if we feel this when we are trained up from infancy amidst influences and exhortations reminding us that it is our duty to try to rise above the level of society, how much more must the Corinthians have felt it when this idea of moral elevation had been presented new to them after they were grown to mature age, and still more after the voice of their first teacher was withdrawn from them and they were left to struggle alone!

Again, we have grown up amid an atmosphere and spirit in society and in education which Christianity has created. Even those who now strenuously resist Christianity cannot, if they would, free themselves from what it has planted in them and fashioned around them. In fact, they do not wish to free themselves, for they have never realized that they owe to Christianity much of what they most value in themselves, and especially that they owe to it the spirit which leads them to regard religion from the moral point of view and to probe and test it as a moral influence.

But those converts from paganism were suddenly brought into

contact with this Christian spirit as a novelty. Nothing in their experience had prepared them for it. They were beginning to attempt to live a life which had to rest upon a totally new and strange basis of thought and ideas and philosophy. The need for some such basis was forced even on the least thoughtful among them. In the present time many of us contrive to pass through life without thinking much about the philosophy on which our life and conduct rest; but that is due to the fact that, in our early training and amid the pressure of society and education and home influences, some such philosophic basis has been made part of our nature by so insensible a process that many of us never become conscious that we are practical philosophers. We solve the philosophic problem by walking where we have been taught to walk, and never know that we have been solving it.

But it was different in Corinth, where the incongruity between their old mental equipment and the conduct which they were now aiming at was constantly forced upon the new converts. They must think: they must try to frame some scheme to coordinate their life: they must try in a groping, blind, tentative way to make a new philosophy fitted to their new life. Yet their old ideas and ways of thinking could not be easily got rid of, and were constantly liable to cause them perplexity where they tried to reason about life and conduct. In many practical questions—where we will unconsciously and unintelligently choose the right way because we do what our mothers taught us from infancy—the new converts, if they acted unconsciously and unintelligently, doing what they had learned from infancy, would choose the wrong way; and the only method by which they could enter on the right way was by conscious, deliberate choice. It is always easy to err: it was doubly easy for the Corinthians to err, when they were trying to reason about the right course in many of the situations in which they might daily be placed. Yet they must reason and weigh arguments about matters which afterwards were gradually settled by the experience and errors of generations. They were beginning to put together in practice the first planks of the platform on which Christian society should rest, or rather to try how much of the existing pagan platform could be used and how much must be destroyed before a Christian society became possible.

Slowly a new fabric was built up. Names, forms of politeness, social customs, methods of address, and so on, in time became settled in Christian forms, partly inherited with little or no change from pagan society, partly remade in substitution for rejected parts of the old pagan fabric. The older forms had been leavened deeply with paganism and the question was continually forcing itself on every Christian's attention, how far might he use forms that had some pagan association without thereby expressing veneration for pagan deities and ideas? At what point must he draw the line and cease to use those forms and ideas? The answer was often most perplexing.

For example, take the mere question of names. Was it permissible for Christians to bear names connected with heathen gods? If a Christian answered to the name Demetrios, Dionysodoros, Menophantos, did he thereby profess respect for Demeter, Dionysos, or Men? The answer here was comparatively easy, and yet it was not uniform. It was not necessary to proscribe such names. Yet many of them passed—some quickly, some slowly—out of Christian use, while some acquired new associations: Dionysos and Demetrios ceased to suggest the pagan gods, and only reminded Christians of the saints so named. Many new and purely Christian names were introduced, for example, Anastasios, Agape, Renatus, Kyriakos, etc. Others, which were rare or not extremely common among the pagans, such as Elpis, Eirene, Sozomenos and Sozomene, became fashionable among the Christians.[1]

But that is one of the simplest questions that were daily presented to the Corinthians for a decision. Amid these difficulties they would long for the presence of an authorized teacher; and we can well understand that they mentioned in their letter to Paul how much, after his departure, they appreciated Apollos' work among them, and how they were eager for his return to them (16:12).

Professor Findlay has well expressed in his restoration of their letter the feeling of the Corinthians on this subject;[2] and he has rightly apprehended the bearing of Acts 18:27–28 on the situation in Corinth. Apollos' work in Corinth "helped them much who had believed." As usual, Luke's history placards before us, as it were in big letters,[3] the one most critical fact: Apollos came in rather to help the existing converts in their need than to make new converts.

We need not therefore wonder that the Corinthians philosophized, and suggested to St. Paul plans for regenerating society. They were bound to do so. Nor need we wonder if they were just a little too well pleased with their own plans. The young philosopher is generally pleased with his new scheme of life; and the young reformer is generally confident that he is on the point of restoring purity, and with it happiness, to humanity. Still less should we sneer at the mistakes that they made, even the backslidings and crimes that they did not succeed in avoiding, as if these showed that their new religion had failed to affect them. The greatest miracle in history is the way in which the lofty simplicity of Christianity entered the heart of such a world as that of Corinth in spite of the deadening power of society and education. Those who most study contemporary life in the Greco-Roman world will most wonder at the miracle.

28

Meat of Sacrificed Animals

One of the difficulties constantly besetting the new converts in a city like Corinth was whether they ought to eat the flesh of animals that had been offered in sacrifice to a pagan deity. The ordinary sacrifice among the Greeks was not burned: only the inedible parts of the animal were given to the gods, while the useful meat was eaten. Much of the flesh that was set on the table in private houses, or that was exposed for sale in the market, had been cut from the sacrificial victims. Had it thereby become polluted? Could the person who ate it be considered to be assisting, as a sort of accessory after the fact, in sacrificing to an idol?

The Apostolic Decree in Acts 15:29 had ordered the converts in the province of Syria-Cilicia to abstain from such meat; and Paul himself had impressed this duty also on his Galatian churches (Acts 16:4). Considering how emphatically he speaks in this epistle of the uniformity of his teaching in all the churches (1 Cor. 7:17), one can hardly avoid the conclusion that he had delivered also to the Corinthian church "the decrees to keep."

But when this order came to be carried out, it involved many difficulties. Was the Christian bound to inquire carefully and find out whether every piece of meat offered for sale in a shop was sacrificial? If he omitted to ask, and bought and ate such meat, had he been guilty of sin? If he asked and received false information, which led him to eat such meat, was he guilty of sin? If he were eating in the house of a non-Christian friend or relative, was he bound to ask about the previous history of every dish on the table, outraging all courtesy thereby, and often putting questions which the host would be really unable to answer? Such practical difficulties would meet the Corinthian Christians frequently, unless they went out of the world and lived entirely separate from surrounding society, thereby losing all opportunity of influencing their neighbors.

Evidently the Corinthians put these and similar difficulties before Paul, and indicated their answer. They could not accept the Apostolic Decree as right in this point. It was contrary to the knowledge, the discernment of moral truth (γνῶσις), which they felt in their own heart and conscience.[1] They all perceived with inevitable and overpowering certainty that an idol was nothing. How could a piece of meat become unclean through the influence of that which was nothing? The idol had neither existence nor power, and could not affect the meat. It would therefore be absurd and irrational to act as if the idol could harm the meat. No, it would even be wrong so to act, for it would be a practical teaching of the false doctrine, that these false gods possess real existence and power whereas we know that no idol is anything in the world, and that there is no God but one.

In answer Paul, of course, did not quote the Apostolic Decree. They knew it, and their knowledge had only led them to controvert its orders. In fact the decree formed the text of the present discussion.

Moreover, it would be worse than useless to refer those young philosophers—bent on thinking for themselves and understanding all things, proud of their own capacity for discerning moral truth—to a formal decree. They must feel the truth spring from their own mind, not have it given to them by external authority.

And so Paul proceeds to expound the philosophic basis on which that prohibition in the Apostolic Decree rested. The Christian society must be built up upon mutual sympathy and courtesy. The brother must not merely be courteous to his pagan host. He must also be courteous to his hesitating, doubtful, scrupulous, not very strong or discerning Christian brother. This true courtesy comes only through sympathy and love. The pure intellectual discernment of truth might only make them self-confident and unsympathetic toward their brethren.

After the preceding remarks were in print I observed how admirably Professor R. J. Knowling has expressed the same thought in his recent edition of Acts: "St. Paul's language in 1 Cor. viii. 1–13, x. 14–22, Rom. xiv., may fairly be said to possess the spirit of the Decree, and to mark the discriminating wisdom of one 'eager to lead his disciples behind the rule to the principle.' "[2]

Formerly, the Apostolic Decree seemed to me a compromise;[3] and from a certain point of view it may be called a compromise; but that point of view is external and unintelligent. The Decree was really the brief practical expression of the sympathetic fellow-feeling which ought to bind together the two elements in the Christian church, Gentile and Jew; but it stated only the result, and

St. Paul now explains to the Corinthians the moral grounds on which it was based.

I might here reproduce almost entirely the excellent paper of Professor W. Lock on this chapter (*Expositor* [July 1897] 66ff.); but it is the shorter way to ask the reader to turn to those pages. Only on one serious point might a modification be desired in his exposition. He says that "the reason why St. Paul does not quote the Decree" is that "the circumstances had changed." I think we have seen a more satisfactory reason: the decree is not quoted because it is the topic under discussion. It is exactly as in the epistle to the Galatians. Scholars have argued that, since the Apostolic Council and Decree are not mentioned elsewhere in that epistle, they must be meant in 2:1–10. But they are not mentioned, because they are the main topic of controversy: they are burning in the minds of all parties, and hence they are not formally appealed to.

29

Officials in the Corinthian Church

In view of the situation described in chapter 27 the provision of permanent officers and guides among the Corinthians was also urgently necessary. In Acts nothing is recorded of any such provision as regards Corinth. But it has been pointed out[1] that when the author of Acts mentions the institution of officials by Paul in his first churches, and when the existence of officials is elsewhere implied in many of the later churches such as Ephesus, Philippi, and Thessalonica, though their appointment is not mentioned in Acts, all who appreciate the methodical expression of Luke must infer that the first case is intended to be typical of the appointments made in all later cases. Paul directed that officials should be appointed in every church, and prescribed a method which involved voting of the congregation under the direction and precedence of some apostolic representative, who had considerable powers to instruct the body of voters as to method and probably to reject unsuitable names. See Titus 1:5–7 and 1 Timothy 3.

Some scholars, indeed, consider that the absence of any reference to *presbyteroi* in this epistle is a sufficient proof that none were instituted in Corinth. The silence is perhaps a sufficient proof that the institution had in Corinth failed in its purpose; and the ill-success may be traced in such passages as 11:21 and 14:26ff.; but it cannot prove that no officers had been appointed, in view of two passages.

1. In 9:28 "helpings, governings," must be taken as an expression equivalent to "officers to help the poor, and direct the business of the congregation," and it is clear that all the kinds of personages there enumerated, from "apostles" to "tongues," were known in the Corinthian church. There were therefore in that church officers charged with certain administrative duties.

2. In 9:12 it is clearly implied that there were persons receiving

salaries or maintenance from the church in Corinth;[2] and Paul claims an equal right to receive maintenance: "if others partake of this right over you, do not we yet more?" It seems impossible to suppose that the right was conceded to unauthorized and merely volunteer teachers and speakers. The right of maintenance by the church involves formal recognition and appointment of those persons by the church.

The influence from those passages is plain. There were in the Corinthian church paid officials charged with administrative duties. These can hardly have been chosen except from among the seniors and men of experience; but the name *presbyteroi*, "elders," does not seem to have been applied to them in Corinth. Titles were, at first, determined in the church more by local usage and language than by a formal and universal rule. Now the word *presbyteroi*, as a title, was not much used in Greece, but it was common in Asia Minor.

The inscriptions are clear on that point. *Presbyteroi* are mentioned in many parts of Asia Minor as members of a body possessed of a high social standing and something of an official character. That body was commonly called the *gerousia*, but its members were spoken of at Chios, Cos, Iasos, Ephesus, Smyrna, Philadelphia, Magnesia ad Meandrum, and many other places, as the *presbyteroi*; in Eumenea and Hieropolis as the *geraioi*,[3] and the entire body was occasionally mentioned as the *synedrion* or *systema* of the *presbyteroi*. Thus the Christians of that country were accustomed to regard the name *presbyteros* as a noun, implying something of rank, standing, age, and even official position; and it was readily applied to the body of persons selected as elders, experienced and trusty, to manage the business of the congregation. But in Greece proper and in Macedonia the word *presbyteros* was hardly used except as an adjective, "older," and conveyed none of the meaning that people in Asia Minor associated with it as a noun.[4]

A parallel variation is seen in early Christian usage. Clement to the Corinthians distinguished *presbyteroi* as "elderly men" from the *hegoumenoi* ("officials") in Corinth (1.3), and from *proëgoumenoi* in Rome (21.6). In Thessalonica Paul mentions the *proïstamenoi*, in Philippi the *episkopoi*. In the cities of Lycaonia and eastern Phrygia (i.e., south Galatia), Luke mentions *presbyteroi*, as he does also in Jerusalem. In Ephesus the names *episkopoi* and *presbyteroi* are both used.[5] *Prostamenos* is used in an early Phrygian Christian inscription (of the fourth century probably); and the term *geraioi* was perhaps used in Eumenea, *proëdroi* in Hierapolis.[6] Thus even in districts where the term *presbyteros* was known it was not uncommon for persons who paid some attention to style and accuracy of Greek to use a more correct Greek word. *Presbyteros* as a title was felt to be a little slangy, and was tabooed by purists.

The most correct Greek usage evidently was a participle, such as *hegoumenoi* or *proïstamenoi*, "the leading men," "the prominent ones." Luke never uses these words, but only *presbyteroi*,[7] for he employed the popular language of Asia Minor and the Aegean coasts, and elsewhere his tendency to a less polished tone in matters of name and title than Paul has been pointed out.[8] Thus we find everywhere in the Pauline churches officials of the same general type, but not always called by the same title. They were chosen and paid by the church.

It is therefore highly probable that there were in Corinth such officials, called afterwards, apparently, *hegoumenoi*.[9] Paul himself mentions them only under the very general and abstract title "governings," probably because the title was not as yet fixed, and usage varied so widely.

Yet there is nowhere even the faintest sign in Paul's reply that the Corinthians had referred to them in their letter. This is all the more remarkable inasmuch as a different class of persons were prominently mentioned in that letter, namely, the volunteer speakers in the assembly, the prophets and speakers with tongues, who rose as the Spirit prompted them.

In his reconstruction Professor Findlay brings out well that the Corinthians laid much stress on the services and the work of those volunteers in their church, and that they congratulated themselves much on the forwardness and zeal shown by so many of their members in guiding and instructing the congregation, so that the "difficulty is to find a hearing for all whom the Spirit prompts (14:26 ff.)." It is all very naive, very interesting, so characteristic of a young community, and, above all, of a community consisting mainly of Greeks, who are never eager to obey the constituted authority, but always forward to govern themselves and to direct their neighbors.

But certainly the silence of Paul about the influence of those officials in Corinth is noteworthy. He nowhere bids the Corinthians obey them. Yet it is plain that one of the most serious faults which Paul saw among the Corinthians was insubordination, and that there was hardly any advice which they stood more in need of than "obey them that are in authority among you." Must we not infer that the existing officials in Corinth had been unsuccessful, that they had given way to the same faults as the congregation generally, that they were in some degree responsible for fomenting the spirit of argument and criticism and partisanship, which was such a dangerous factor in Corinthian life, that it was they who had condoned the conduct of the worst offender? It was hardly possible simply to advise the Corinthians to obey their *hegoumenoi*. But a guarded counsel is given in the concluding paragraph, when Paul gathers up in brief the most urgent teaching of the epistle, and beseeches the Corinthians to "be in subjection unto such" (16:16) as Stephanas and his household, who "have set themselves to minister to the saints" (v. 15); and further, to be in subjection "to everyone who helps in the work and labors" (v. 16). Those who do the work should have the obedience of the congregation, which doubtless implies that there are some who have failed to do the work.

The question which has sometimes been put, if *presbyteroi* were purely administrative officials or if they took part in teaching and preaching, would have seemed meaningless and absurd to the Christians of that time. The idea that there could be persons eminent in the congregation who did not teach was inconceivable then. Stephen and Philip were among the seven appointed "to serve tables" (Acts 6:2ff.); but their conspicuous position gave them only greater advantage to "help in the work and labor."

30

Eating in an Idol Temple (8:10)

In chapter 28 we described some of the difficulties which were caused to all the early Christians by the question whether meats sacrificed to false gods had become polluted thereby and so rendered unfit for Christian use. Before completing the subject, however, it was necessary to examine whether the widely accepted view that no officials had as yet been appointed in the Corinthian church was correct; and we found reason to think (1) that there were officials at Corinth corresponding to the *presbyteroi* in the Galatian churches (Acts 14:20), but not called by that name; and (2) that some of those officials had been guilty of practices which Paul disapproved of, and that therefore he refrained from recommending the congregation to be obedient to them in 1 Corinthians 16. Our view is that the *hegoumenoi* (to use the descriptive participle, "leading [men]," which was probably the nearest approach to a title yet in use for the Corinthian officials) had taken a course which Paul strongly disapproved of by continuing to be members of pagan clubs or societies in Corinth.

We may take it for granted that the letter of the Corinthians to Paul had been drawn up by a small number of persons, and not by the whole congregation. It may have been—and we think that it was—submitted to the whole body of the congregation after it was composed; but a letter could hardly be composed except by one or a few persons. Doubtless the composers were the leading officials, for the writing of letters on behalf of the congregation, which was probably entrusted at an early date to the bishop,[1] was an important duty in the early times of the church, since the unity and solidarity of the parts scattered over different lands and cities could be maintained only through visits and correspondence. Such an important part of the church's life would naturally be put in the hands of the officials selected by the church.

The *hegoumenoi*, in drawing up the letter, had included under the general title of "eating meats offered to idols" certain connected practices; and while they defended their right to eat such meats, they evidently intended that their defense should be taken as carrying with it the right to another far more serious kind of action, namely, taking part in societies united by common rites and meals (see chapter 31). We do not mean that the *hegoumenoi* consciously smuggled in the more serious action under the guise of mere eating of sacrificial meat. But they were evidently in the letter defending their own action, and they did so on the ground that the essential fact in it was merely the eating of meat which had been sacrificed, and if they proved the latter to be permissible, they established their right in the more serious matter. Paul finds it necessary to distinguish mere eating of sacrificial meats from that more serious action, pronouncing the one to be allowable (except insofar as sympathy for the feelings of other Christians made it right to abstain), while showing that the other is actual idolatry.

The real nature of the Corinthians' action first appears in 8:10: "If a man sees you who have knowledge sitting at meat in a place of an idol" (εἰδώλιον). These words arrest our attention: some of the Christians were to be seen taking part in a feast or banquet in some place, a temple or other building, consecrated to a pagan deity. What is the precise meaning of this?

The form of statement in 8:10 is remarkable: "you who have knowledge sitting in an idol place." The way in which one person is apostrophized suggests that someone of those who had written to him is singled out as the guilty party, or rather that several such persons are appealed to one by one. That implies that one or more of the *hegoumenoi* had been seen in an idol's temple and been talked about in the congregation.

The feast must necessarily have had the form of a ceremony connected with the worship of the deity to whom the locality was consecrated. On this there can be no question. A feast in such a locality could not be a purely secular and nonreligious function. Yet it seems hardly possible that a professing Christian could take part in a pagan ceremony, ostensibly religious, publicly and before the eyes of the world, while still remaining a professed member of the church. Even if he desired to remain so, it is inconceivable that he should have been permitted by the brethren to remain among them unquestioned.

We cannot accept the suggestion that the action of those who sat in an idol's temple was due to bravado, as "a thing done to show their 'knowledge' and freedom from superstition about the idol."

We have been led to form a different conception of the character of the Corinthians (see especially chapter 27), which makes it clear to us that the nature of the ceremony must have been such that the religious aspect could easily be regarded by them as secondary and comparatively unimportant. The nature of ancient Greek religion and its relation to ordinary social institutions and associations explains the difficulty.

31

The Corinthian Clubs or Associations

Associations or clubs of private individuals were very common in the Greek cities. They often were constituted for some non-religious purpose. They were sometimes benefit societies or burial societies. They might be intended for some useful municipal end: for example, the body of 150 firemen, which, as Pliny reports to Trajan in *Epistle* 33, it was proposed to form at Nicomedia in Bithynia, would certainly have taken the form of an association bound together by the common worship of a divinity. They would have held their meetings in a place consecrated to that divinity, and feasts in the form of ceremonies of their cult would have been celebrated. Hence Trajan refused to permit the formation of the body of firemen. He knew that they must be a society, and he knew how liable such societies were in Greek cities to be turned into political clubs or to be diverted to the purpose of vying with, and ultimately quarreling with, other clubs. And as Bithynian cities had suffered much from such internal quarrels, he was afraid that even a body of firemen would turn into a cause of disorder.

The attitude which an emperor of such fair and practical mind and lofty views as Trajan, who governed his action on general principles, took up towards a proposed association of firemen is eminently instructive in view of the Corinthian situation. Pliny, who knew well what Trajan's general principle was, pleaded for an exception in this case: only real workmen should be admitted, and the number should be limited to 150. But Trajan replied that the body of workmen would soon turn into a *hetairia*, a body of *hetairoi* or pledged comrades, who would feel their bond to one another stronger than their obedience to the law.

Again, in Corinth there were many strangers, resident for purposes of business. The strangers who belonged by origin to any one country or large city would form a society for purposes of mutual help and intercourse and enjoyment. And this society would be constituted as a religious association for worshiping some deity, generally the patron of their country or city. So at Puteoli the Syrians from Berytus met in the worship of a god whom they called in Latin Jupiter, but who was undoubtedly a Syrian god, called in a Latin inscription by the Latin name Jupiter Heliopolitanus, that is, the Baal of Heliopolis (Baalbek). There must have been many such societies at Corinth; and they would greatly conduce to the pleasure and comfort of their members.

Das griechische Vereinswesen by Dr. E. Ziebarth may be consulted by those who desire to gain some clearer conception of the extent and variety of such associations in Greek cities. The descendants of some ancient family might form themselves into a society with a common cult. Companies for trading purposes or for farming taxes, groups of traders engaged in the same line of business, groups of persons occupied in the pursuit of knowledge, companies of artists and actors or men of letters, political clubs, and a host of other associations can be traced in the cities of the eastern provinces. Many of these can be proved to have met in the performance of a common worship; many others are too obscure to admit of positive assertion; but probably all relied on a similar religious bond. It is highly probable that many societies, which Dr. Ziebarth classes as formed purely for religious ends, served also some purpose of ordinary life,[1] though we have no evidence[2] of that side of their character. In the names of some societies, whose main purpose was nonreligious, the religious character was so strongly expressed that their real character might easily escape notice.

Owing doubtless to the want of epigraphic memorials of Corinth, Dr. Ziebarth has found no reference to any club in that city except in a passage of Suidas, which seems to describe a Corinthian Society of Kotys, of the worst character. It was apparently a purely religious society, and was called by the characteristic title θίασος.

But there can be no doubt that Corinth was a favorable soil for the growth of associations and clubs of every kind. Where the population was homogeneous and simple in character, such societies were less numerous and flourishing. It was in great centers of international life and commercial intercourse, such as the harbors of Piraeus and Rhodes, that societies flourished most:[3] and Corinth, after its restoration by Julius Caesar, was the greatest international center of Greece. Incidentally we observe in this characteristic a proof that the societies were an influence hostile to the unity of the state, and therefore to patriotism and national order; and we understand why patriots and lawgivers disliked and condemned them.

The more united the state, the weaker the societies in it; the more mixed the state, the stronger the clubs.

The more we study Greek city life the more obvious becomes the extreme importance of the question, whether Christians might join in the common meals which constituted a leading feature in the ceremonial binding each of those clubs into a unity. If they joined in those meals, they must eat meat which they had seen sacrificed to idols.

But as society was constituted in the cities of the Greco-Roman world, they must either join in those meals or leave the societies, excellent and useful as many of them were. Doubtless some, and even many, of the Christians had belonged in their pagan days to such societies. Doubtless some of the *hegoumenoi* were active members and even leading spirits in them. They had paid the subscriptions (which were a regular feature of such associations): were they to lose all benefit therefrom? Worse than that, were they to retire from those in which the objects were really praiseworthy and beneficial? If so, then, as they said in their letter to Paul, they could find no place for themselves in the world and must go out of it.[4]

There can be no doubt what view the Corinthian officials were, as a body, disposed to take on this subject. They would remain in the ordinary associations which had mainly a nonreligious purpose. They would partake of the common meals made on the flesh of victims sacrificed to the god in whose worship the association met, and served in his holy place; and they justified this on the ground that the idol was nothing. They doubtless reminded Paul that he himself had often declared to them that an idol was nothing, a mere stock or stone, devoid of all life and power, having no real existence; and they drew the conclusion that meat offered to nothing could not derive any pollution therefrom. The meat intended to be eaten remained after the sacrifice exactly the same as before.

This was probably the most serious matter in the present situation of the Corinthians, and Paul's method of dealing with it is instructive and beautiful. The right to be members of pagan clubs had not been directly submitted to him; and he does not treat it as if it had. He refrains from imposing any absolute prohibition or stating any dogmatic rule, which might be like a law constraining the free action of the individual Christian. Especially, in dealing with the Corinthian philosophers, it would be worse than useless to impose a prohibition on them. It was necessary to lead them to place on themselves a prohibitory law.

This was not a case like the crime alluded to in chapter 5, in regard to which an absolute law must be stated. It was a case where something—and even a good deal—must be left to the individual conscience. And so Paul tries to lead his correspondents up to a higher plane of thought, on which they can see more clearly all that was involved in the question, and may judge for themselves. That higher plane of thought, on which alone they could see clearly and judge rightly, required among them a far better appreciation of the common bond that united the brethren. Hence he diverges from the topic for a time, while he tries to work up his readers to appreciate some sides of the situation which were as yet hid from them, and then returns to it in chapter 10.

32

The Common Meal (10:14–21)

The central point in the ceremonial that bound together the members of those Greek associations or clubs was the common meal, and especially the common cup. "I have eaten out of the holy dish, I have drunk from the sacred cup" was the sacred formula pronounced by each participator in the Mysteries,[1] which may be taken as typical of the whole class of associations.

It is important to notice the analogy between the great mysteries and the associations. The religious associations were simply private societies of *mystai*, celebrating the rites and mysteries of a special deity. Even the associations for a nonreligious purpose also tended towards a similar close fellowship—to become bodies of *hetairoi*, as Trajan said—and modeled their religious ritual (so far as evidence goes) after the mysteries, so that the members became *symmystai*, that is, persons initiated in the same mystic ritual. In one case in a club at Smyrna, the members are styled both *symbiotai* (i.e., associates)[2] and *symmystai*.[3]

It is hardly possible to use too strong language in describing the strength and closeness of the tie which bound together those pagan societies. It was a power often stronger than the tie of country or of blood, and was considered by the wiser pagans to be a real danger to the healthy and free life of society.

Prudent lawgivers recognized in the common meal of the societies the special bond of union which might make them dangerous to the state by leading the members to regard their unity and fellowship in the society as more binding than their unity and patriotism in the nation. And it is a well-known fact that it was the common meal (the *Agape*) of the early Christians which most of all roused the suspicion of the imperial Roman governor, and that this was probably the reason why the *Agape* was soon generally given up by the church.

All those persons, then, who participated in the common meal of the pagan society are initiated into the mystic bond of union, and enter into communion with one another through the power, not divine but demonic, which constitutes and gives strength to that mystic bond. Behind the idol to which the pagan society sacrifices is a certain demonic power; and those who participate in the sacrificial feast become united in a mystic union with that power and with one another.

In this opinion as to the importance of the sacrificial meal Paul was stating what was at that time generally accepted. The meal was regarded not merely as the eating of food in common, but as an act involving real conveyance of power. To take an illustrative example, the belief has always been widespread and strong in the East that the stranger who succeeds in entering (even by craft and stealth) within the circle of the family religion and partaking of the family meal becomes to such a degree part of the family that his person is sacred to all its members. He must not be injured by them; and though he may have slain one of their number previously, yet revenge must give way to the bond which now unites him to the family.

Evidently Paul's view is that membership in those pagan societies, beneficial and excellent as some of them were, was irreconcilable with the Christian spirit, and the reason lay in the common meal and the power it exerted on the mind and nature of the participants, making them all into brothers.[4]

But while the sacrificial meal becomes a force in the mind of those who share in it, it is also clear that the force arises through the surrounding circumstances and ceases when it is divorced from them. The power behind the idol is not a self-existent devil, as Justin and Tertullian and the early church in general crudely imagined. It is a power relative to the human mind, and conditioned by the whole series of facts that play upon the mind. If the same meat is carried to another place, a butcher's shop or a private house, and eaten in different surroundings, apart from the company which uses that rite to cement its fellowship, then it is no longer affected by the demonic power; it has suffered nothing, but remains clean.

Must we not conclude, then, that the danger which Paul dreads in the pagan societies was the formation of a tie of brotherhood inconsistent with and opposed to the tie of Christian union? Intercourse with pagans is not forbidden; one may mix in ordinary society, even though one knows that the pagan does not obey those principles of pure life which the Christians must comply with. One may do business with pagans, accept their invitations, eat and drink with them; but one should not bind oneself to them by the tie of a common solemn ritual, which exercises a strong constraining force on the will and nature of man, and prevents him from real devotion to Christ.

33

The Pagan Clubs and the Christian Church

If we are to estimate the importance attached to a topic in Paul's mind, as he was writing, by the comparative frequency with which the words connected with it occur in his letter, then it is beyond question that "idolatry" was a topic that occupied much of his thought as he wrote this letter to the Corinthians.

The words, "idol," "idolatry," etc. (εἴδωλον and its connections, εἰδώλιον, εἰδωλόθυτος, εἰδωλολάτρης, εἰδωλολατρεία) occur fifteen times in 1 Corinthians, six times in the remaining letters, and eleven times in the rest of the New Testament. Contrast this with the word πόρνη and its connections. These occur twelve times in 1 Corinthians, seven times in the remaining letters, and thirty-five times in the rest of the New Testament. Now we have pointed out that the common view of commentators—who describe impurity as the great enemy and danger in Corinth—is mistaken (see chapter 20), and that the danger on that side was common to all ancient society and rose from the low ideas prevalent on the subject among even the most enlightened and orderly class of society. The danger that bulked most largely in Paul's mind as he wrote to the Corinthians was not impurity (though of course that was everywhere a danger in the pagan world), but idolatry.

They were still a very young congregation. The prime need was to raise them quite out of their idolatrous upbringing and surroundings; and the most serious danger was lest they should unwittingly and unconsciously fall back into the practices connected with idolatry. But observe: the danger was not that they should directly return to the worship of the gods whom they had abandoned. In that case they would have been hopeless, and their "last state would be worse than the first." The danger was lest, while they thought they were still leading the Christian life, they should be attempting to combine with it practices and acts which were irreconcilable with it and must destroy their Christian spirit.

Now Paul tends to connect together the thought of idolatry and the thought of the holy sacrament. They must be related to one another as the evil and the antidote: between them there could be no other connection. If we glance at the sequence of thought in 10:14–21, the close connection of the two ideas in the apostle's mind is unmistakable: "the cup of the Lord and the cup of *daimonia*," "the table of the Lord and the table of *daimonia*," are side by side in his mind and words. When he begins the paragraph, "My beloved, flee from idols," he continues at once, "I speak as to men who can understand: judge what I say. The cup of blessing which we bless, is it not a communion and fellowship in the blood of Christ?" And throughout the paragraph he balances the one idea against the other, and passes back and forward between the two.

It is impossible to read that paragraph without being impressed by Paul's obvious intention to set these two facts, the eucharistic meal and the common meal of the pagan societies, before the minds of the Corinthians as two hostile ideas, two irreconcilable and mutually destructive forces: "You cannot drink the cup of the Lord and the cup of demonic powers; you cannot partake of the table of the Lord and the table of demonic powers."

The word "communion" or "fellowship" (κοινωνία) determines the sense of this passage. It does not simply indicate that the celebrants of the sacrificial feast each eat some of the food that has been consecrated by sacrifice. Its fundamental force is to express "fellowship" and "close union with each other." The fellowship is cemented in virtue of the common meal, not through the dividing of the food among the participants, but through the common enjoyment by them of the same meal with all that is implicated in the meal, namely, the demonic power communicated by its having been offered in sacrifice amid certain impressive surroundings.

The word κοινωνία is often applied to the close mystic union between husband and wife, and the first formation of that union was guaranteed and sanctioned by the common partaking of the mystic cup, as has been shown elsewhere; and the ceremony was in various respects adopted from the ritual of the Mysteries.[1] The uniting bond in the religiously constituted pagan societies was conceived as similar in strength and character.

The force of Paul's assertion here is not fully realized until one takes it in conjunction with what he is denying. As we have seen, the Corinthian philosophers argued that the sacrifice, being offered to a thing of nothing, could not suffer any pollution or come under any influence from that nonentity; and that they who possessed insight might as freely partake of sacrificial meat as of similar meat which had not been sacrificed. Paul accepts part, and denies part of their assertion. Such meat of a sacrifice may be freely eaten, when it has been bought as exposed for sale in a butcher's shop (10:25). The meat in itself does not suffer anything from the thing of nothing, the idol. But the evil lies in the fellowship and communion with others in virtue of the common meal forming the climax of the common performance of the idolatrous ritual; for in those surroundings the participant binds and pledges himself to his fellows in association with demonic powers.

Further, even the eating of that sacrificial meat is harmless when it is offered to a guest in a private house (evidently included is even the house of someone who sacrificed at a temple, and brought away the meat to his own house). The meat in itself is not unclean or polluted; and the circumstances are no longer such as to give any ritual force to the participating in it. In fact, the eater now simply takes his part of the meat; and in the act of eating he does not enter into communion with the other participants.

Still, even in such a situation the sympathy and love of the guest will lead him to refrain, if another of the brethren, less robust in conscience and penetrating in insight, points out to him—in horror and deprecation (as is implied)—that the meat before him has been part of a sacrifice. But in this case, it is only sympathy for his brother, and not the nature of the case in itself that leads him to refrain.

34

The Imperial Policy and the Pagan Clubs

In order to complete the subject, it is necessary to notice certain difficulties and objections which may perhaps be suggested in reference to the interpretation advocated in chapters 31–33; and the consideration of these will at the same time bring out more clearly the nature of the question involved and its great importance in early Christian history.

We have seen in chapter 31 that Trajan in particular, and the imperial policy generally, were opposed to the associations. How then could these be so numerous and so strong as we have represented? Considering how much stress we have laid on the analogy between the Pauline and the imperial attitude toward the associations, this objection must be examined.

The imperial government might regard the clubs with disfavor. It might forbid or restrict the formation of new associations, when the proposal was formally laid before it (as in the case quoted under Trajan's reign); but it was out of its power to destroy all associations, nor was the attempt ever made.

Julius Caesar and Augustus had seen in the great civil wars that the centers of disturbance and the chief causes of disorder lay in the political clubs. Hence they discouraged them and dissolved many in Rome, examining all and allowing those only to continue that rested on positive enactments by the state or on prescriptive right. The most recently formed had been the most dangerous; and the imperial policy watched jealously over the institution of new clubs. The Senate scrutinized each case for a new club, and gave permission only after receiving imperial authorization (*Auctoritas Augusti*). The necessary condition was that the new society must serve some useful purpose in the state. As all clubs had a religious character, each being bound together in the rites of a common worship, the Senate, as holding the control over the public religion, had to be consulted.

Moreover, the tendency to form associations was far too deep-rooted in Greco-Roman society to be eradicated by even the imperial power. No government can change the ingrained customs and ways of living among a people. The spread of Greco-Roman civilization, which was the unvarying aim of the imperial policy, carried with it the institution of the clubs. It was where that civilization was least influential, where rusticity and ignorance and orientalism were supreme, that the clubs were least important. Greco-Roman society was hardly possible without clubs. A revolution in the customs of society was needed before clubs could be abolished. Augustus, therefore, preferred to take this essential feature of society into the service of the state: it was a powerful element in society, and might be used to serve his purposes. Now one of his aims was to renovate and strengthen the religious spirit in the state. This he could not achieve, as ancient society was constituted, except through the clubs. The spread of an ancient religion always proceeded through the institution of clubs to practice the worship in new places. Thus Augustus spread his new state religion—the worship of Rome and the emperor as the god incarnate in human form on the earth. He founded associations which met in the practice of the state religion, and in that way he enlisted them in the support of his policy. So, for example, he formed those clubs in the Italian towns called *Augustales*, or *Cultores Augusti*.

In the same way the religions of the East spread over the Greek and Roman world under the form of religious clubs or associations (*collegia*). The synagogues of the Jews and the congregations of the early Christians were inevitably regarded by the pagans as clubs for the practice of religion. Lucian (*Peregrinus* 11) calls a Christian congregation a θίασος or religious association; and Celsus (*contra Celsus* 3.23) termed the Christians θιασῶται, members of a religious club.

The early emperors regarded religious clubs with varying mind. Augustus kept Isis outside of Rome. The reason was obviously political: Egypt and Egypt's queen were the great public enemy in the earlier part of his reign. Therefore the religion of Egypt must be kept out. But he permitted the Jews to flourish, and did not exile other religions from Rome. Tiberius was hostile to the Jews and to foreign religions generally, while Caligula was more friendly. Claudius founded the first society of *Dendrophori* in the religion of Cybele; but in his later years he was opposed to the Jews. Nero, under the influence of Poppea, favored the Jews, and his action against the Christians was due to an accidental and personal cause, not to any objection in principle to that class of religious associations.[1] The opinion was formerly entertained also that he founded those loyal clubs called *collegia iuvenum*, which afterwards became so important, connecting the imperial religion with the physical training of young men and the strong human interest involved therein.[2] This institution, however, was in the strictest spirit of the Augustan policy and older than Nero; but he encouraged such clubs.

The whole system of Roman benefit societies, called *collegia tenuiorum*, may perhaps be as old as Augustus. They were permitted to hold monthly meetings for the purpose of a monthly subscription, and such other meetings as they needed for religious purposes. Tertullian (*Apology* 39) says that the Christian congregations also collected monthly subscriptions, not, however, fixed in amount nor obligatory like those in pagan *collegia*, but purely voluntary; and he contrasts the Christian use of the money for charitable purposes with its employment for feasting and sensuality in the pagan clubs.[3]

This sketch brings out clearly how far removed the imperial policy was from abolishing clubs, though Trajan enforced so strictly in Bithynia the general principle that no club dangerous to public peace and order could be permitted, and regarded any new club as an evil or likely to become so. But Bithynia then had been in an exceptional and disturbed condition, and exceptional strictness was needed in preventing or removing all possible causes of disorder.

Yet even in that province Trajan recognized the right of Amisus to maintain its *collegia*, so long as they did not produce dangerous or disorderly results, because Amisus was a free city and enjoyed its own laws. That introduces us to another principle of the imperial policy. In the eastern provinces the emperors did not press the Roman law so strictly as in the west. They allowed the Greek laws great scope.[4] Especially was this the case in the senatorial provinces, such as Asia and Achaia, in which the government was conducted not by the emperor's own representatives, but by officials sent by the Senate.

Only in the case of soldiers was the imperial policy resolute against clubs. No military clubs were permitted. The soldier must not be allowed to come under any bond except that to the emperor nor to belong to any association except his regiment; and the regiment had its own religious bond, the religion of the emperors and the regimental gods.

In fact, while the membership of the clubs was not restricted to the upper classes in society, yet, beyond all doubt, the institution was far more important among those who were at least moderately well off and who made some pretensions to education, good breeding, and knowledge of the world.

The spirit of ancient society was represented in its most concentrated form in the associations. To hold aloof from the clubs was to stamp oneself as a low-class person, as a curmudgeon, almost an enemy of society, alien to every generous impulse and friendly feeling toward neighbors.

The question, then, before St. Paul was whether Christianity could be permitted to grow up in the forms accepted by ancient society, whether it could adapt itself safely to those forms and let them guide[5] its outward social development, or whether it must reject the prevailing forms absolutely. The latter alternative meant, with an energetic and progressive body like the Christians, that they must recreate ancient society after new forms.

In this statement we have the answer to an objection which might be taken to St. Paul's judgment. It might perhaps seem that he was led too far by the analogy which he evidently makes between the common meal of the pagan clubs and the sacrament of the Christians, and that, from an exaggerated and almost superstitious regard for the sanctity of the sacrament, he discouraged any participation in a ceremony which had a strong superficial resemblance to it. But we now see that in this subject there was involved the momentous issue, whether or not it was possible to clothe Christianity in the robes of existing society.

If I may venture on such a subject to state personal impressions, I must confess, on the one hand, that no reconciliation was possible at that time between Christian principles and present social forms. No dispassionate student of history, who refuses to be misled by the glamor and charm of ancient civilization, who studies society as it existed in its reality, can come to any other conclusion.

But, on the other hand, I must also confess that a strong inclination attracts me to the side of those who were trying to effect the reconciliation, and to combine Christian spirit with the existing institutions of society and civilization. That this was impossible we may allow, and yet sympathize with those who were bent on the attempt, and who soon became almost a definite and recognized sect, spread widely among the cities of the Aegean lands, under the title of Nicolaitans.[6]

In another work[7] I have described a similar attempt, made at a later time, when success was not so impossible amid the changed circumstances of the third century. In the scanty evidence the probability seems to be that the first Christian city, the Phrygian Eumenea, had effected successfully such a reconciliation; and that the auspicious result was destroyed in the blood and fire of Diocletian's persecution. But the strength of the Christian feeling among that people, who had gone to considerable lengths in the direction of the old Nicolaitans, was proved by the facts: they all chose death and were burned with their church, "appealing to the God over all."

35

Importance of the Question in the Early Gentile Churches

The subject treated in chapters 30–34 was a most serious question in the development of Christian society and religion. It is of such importance for the New Testament writings and the early Christian times generally that we may profitably follow it further, and notice some other references to it.

It may perhaps have seemed that in chapter 30 we were too hasty when we set aside the theory which explained "sitting in an idol's temple" (1 Cor. 8:10) as referring to participation by Christians in the ordinary regular celebration of the public and recognized pagan ritual. There were afterwards, of course, certain sects which went to great lengths in their attendance upon pagan religious ceremonies; and it might be, and has been, maintained that we have here in germ the principle which was carried out by those later sects. We have, however, been convinced that there was no such fully developed tendency in Corinth to false principle. There was thorough good intention to abide by Paul's teaching in the great principles; and that was absolutely inconsistent with overt participation in idolatrous worship for its own sake.

But, apart from the question whether that interpretation of 8:10 offers a sufficient explanation of the words there used and the situation there described, it can hardly be doubted that that interpretation does not suit the paragraph 10:14–22, which obviously alludes to the same acts of Corinthian Christians. Let us consider that paragraph fairly in its context.

An explanatory paragraph (10:1–11) leads up to it. The experiences of the Jews our fathers are intended to be an example, so that we Christians may learn wisdom.

1–4: Just as you are now all brought out of paganism and become members of the Christian church, sharing all the opportunities and privileges which it offers, so the whole body of our fathers the Jews were brought out of Egypt and equally favored. They were baptized in sea and cloud, as you have been baptized. They all were fed with spiritual food, and all were given to drink of spiritual drink: as you receive the spiritual food and drink of the sacrament.

5–11: But some of them slipped back into the idolatrous practices of the pagans, and into the impure life of the tribes around them; and were punished with death on that account. Their action and its results are typical for us Christians.

12–13: Take warning from that example. Be not overconfident. You are now tempted, as our fathers were tempted. But God does not permit the temptation to be too strong for you. With the evil and the danger he has given the antidote and preservative; but you must be careful, for the temptation is pressing hard on you.

14: Be careful, then, always to avoid and keep far away from idolatry.

15: I put the case to you as reasoning, prudent men, that you judge for yourselves as to what you should do.

16: The cup of the blessing,[1] over which we say the word of blessing and thanks every time we celebrate the rite—does it not constitute our fellowship in the blood of the Christ? The bread which we break—is it not our fellowship in the body of the Christ?

17: Because the bread (which we share and break and divide) is one, we, the many members, are one body and one brotherhood.

18: Look (you who are the spiritual Israel) at the nation of the Jews (the natural, fleshly Israel): does not their common ritual bind them together in a fellowship whose close cohesion is the marvel of the Greek and Roman world? Is not that intimate union due to their taking part in the common sacrifice?

19: But what is my meaning (you may here object)? Do I mean that an idol is a real thing, or that idol-sacrificed meat is a real category (i.e., different in character from meat not so sacrificed)?

20: Certainly not; but I mean that what the pagans sacrifice, they sacrifice to demonic powers and not to God, and I do not wish that you should enter into a fellowship cemented in and through demonic powers.

21: It is impossible and contradictory to drink the cup of the Lord and the cup of demonic powers, or to partake in the table of the Lord and the table of demonic powers (you must choose one or other).

22: If we try to combine these two mutually contradictory rites, we merely provoke the Lord, who refuses to share with demonic powers in your devotion; and that, of course, we are resolved not to do, are we not? We do not imagine—do we?—that we are stronger than he.

It is peculiarly unfortunate that the critical expression in verse 20, though fully explained in 21, is mistranslated in both the Authorized and the Revised Version, "communion with devils" ("demons," in margin). Canon Evans's notes ought to be carefully read. It follows beyond question from what he says that a pagan ceremony is meant, which was not merely a performance of a religious rite, but was felt to be the cementing of a fellowship or communion in and through a ritual meal. No other explanation of this passage seems possible except that which we have proposed.[2]

Further, our explanation restores consistency, coherence, and reason to Paul's opinions about the eating of sacrificial meat. It is not possible without it to gather any clear conception of what was his position on that question. After apparently protesting in the most vehement and impassioned terms against eating it in 10:20–22, he proceeds in 23ff. to discuss it in a cool and almost indifferent tone, as an act which might be done without hesitation, except that kindly feeling towards some weak and rather painfully scrupulous Christian impels one to abstain from an act which in one's own judgment is quite indifferent. But now we see that Paul is distinguishing two radically different acts: (1) he is resolutely bent against the partaking of the ritual meal of a pagan society, and (2) he regards as a trivial matter the mere eating in ordinary life of the meat of an animal which at a previous time and in different circumstances had been offered to an idol.

As a third argument, we observe that, on our explanation, the disagreement which has often been commented on with astonishment between St. Paul's teaching and the attitude of Revelation on this subject entirely disappears. It has been sometimes thought that the horror of *idolothyta*—meats offered to idols—expressed in Revelation by John is in the sharpest contrast to the easy and almost indifferent tone of Paul; and no satisfactory explanation of the contrast seems possible on the ordinary explanation of his judgment. But on our interpretation John and Paul will be found in perfect harmony on this subject.

As it chanced, I began to write the present section immediately after writing on Sardis, Smyrna, and Thyatira, as the result of a careful study of the seven messages in Revelation 2–3. The atmosphere and spirit of those messages brought out the meaning of Paul's words far more perfectly than I had conceived them when writing the preceding sections of this commentary. The messages to Pergamum and Thyatira seemed to spring out of and to develop logically the opinions expressed by Paul. This demands a special paragraph.

36

St. John and St. Paul on Associations and *Idolothyta*

Like Paul, so John points his treatment of the subject by an example taken from Hebrew history. Revelation 2:14 corresponds to 1 Corinthians 10:1–11, but a marked interval has occurred. The method has become familiar and customary; and what would have been to Paul a type and an example becomes in John's mouth a designation and a category.

Paul might have said, "As Balaam taught how to seduce Israel from the right path, so you are being led astray by false teachers toward the same kind of practices." But John says, "Some of you hold the teaching of Balaam."

Further, we saw that there is the strongest contrast between the first 23 verses and the following 10 verses of 1 Corinthians 10: in 1–23 Paul treats with horror the eating of the ritual pagan meal; in 24–33 he treats certain other forms of eating sacrificial meats with comparative indifference. Now the tone of verses 1–23 is exactly the tone of John in the Revelation. Surely we must infer from this that the question with regard to the actions discussed in 1 Corinthians 10:24–33 was closed forever. Paul's decision was final. The case was no longer up for judgment when the Revelation was written.

But the other class of acts, the sharing in the ritual meals, was still a serious danger. It had to be inveighed against, and denounced in the most uncompromising terms. Ephesus had been well taught, and "hated the works of the Nicolaitans." Smyrna was the most free from fault (thanks greatly to the persecution and poverty which were its lot) of all the churches. But the distant Pergamum and Thyatira, farthest away from St. Paul's teaching, were still in the same danger as Corinth had been when Paul was writing this letter.

In both Pergamum and Thyatira some of the Christians still clung to their membership of the pagan associations and shared in the fellowship of the ritual meal. If that evil were not burned out, the whole loose spirit of pagan society, its impurity and its idolatry, would continue to rule in the congregation.

The question, however, continued to be treated and named from the point of view adopted by the Corinthian officials at the first. It was called the question of *idolothyta*, things offered to idols. But the most serious and grave matter involved in it was whether the Christians might continue to take part in those societies which were united in a fellowship of pagan ritual. A common ritual is a great power over the minds of men; and the three great apostles (see the following chapter) were unanimous in refusing to permit paganism to exercise that power over the minds of the young converts.

Perhaps a new light is thrown by our theory on the words of Revelation 2:22: "Behold I do cast her (Jezebel) into a bed, and them that commit adultery with her into great tribulation." It is usual to take "into a bed" and "into great tribulation" as parallel to one another: the "tribulation" is the lot of her partners; her punishment and that of her children is different. Adultery and πόρνεια here mean "idolatry and the low tone of morals which is inseparable from it."

There seems a distinct awkwardness in this; and the whole sentence (though susceptible of defense) fails to satisfy one's feeling for symmetry and completeness in thought. A different interpretation seems to spring naturally from our view of the action meant. The expression is full of bitter, almost savage irony: "See what a feast I will give them! I set her on a couch (i.e., the couch on which a guest at a banquet reclined), and with her idolatrous partners; and the fare provided for them is—tribulation."[1]

That places us in the midst of the scene in Thyatira. One section of the Christian church clings to the social life of the city. They cannot resolve to cut themselves off entirely from the bright and joyous customs of society: they take them with their idolatrous accompaniments and their sacrificial meals. "But I will give them their festal meal: I throw their mistress and prophetess on a couch at their table, and them along with her, to enjoy—the punishment that I have in store for them."

It is true that the word κλίνη (used in Revelation) has only the sense of 'bed" elsewhere in the New Testament; but there is little opportunity for mentioning a couch at a feast. The custom of reclining at supper was adopted from the Greek and Roman fashion, and became usual in Palestine. People sat in meetings and in the temple, but reclined at meat. The Last Supper was eaten reclining, not sitting, as is clear from the words of Matthew, Mark, and Luke,[2] though even the Revised Version maintains the false translation and uses "sit" (but in the margin the proper term is given). The couch at supper must therefore have been well known; and without doubt the ordinary Greek name κλίνη was used, and the author of Revelation therefore had to employ it if he wished to speak of the couch.

Moreover the question may be asked whether we ought not to take κλίνη as a "couch" in Luke 17:34: "There shall be two men on one couch (at supper); there shall be two women grinding together."

37

St. Peter, St. John, and St. Paul on the Sacrificial Feasts

The description of the false teachers in 2 Peter 2:1–22 contains many traits recalling the doctrine of the Nicolaitans and the followers of Balaam and Jezebel in the Revelation, and also the arguments advanced by the Corinthian officials who wrote to Paul. A glance at that chapter will illuminate the nature of the issues on which Paul had to pronounce judgment in 1 Corinthians 10.

Peter[1] speaks of those teachers in the future tense: "There shall be among you also false teachers." But the whole character of the chapter shows that he is describing a class of teaching which was already powerful among the Christians, while it was likely to grow even more dangerous.

Just as Paul in the opening of 1 Corinthians 10, so Peter begins chapter 2 by quoting as an example and warning the history of the Jews: "There were false prophets also among the people (of Israel)."

The greed and ambition of our false teachers stimulates their teaching: they have personal ends to gain by making themselves the leaders of the congregation and imposing their policy and ways of living on all. But they will be destroyed like the fallen angels, like the ancient world at the flood, like Sodom and Gomorrah, for God can punish the guilty, and especially vicious and unruly persons like them.

10b: They have the qualities characteristic of the richer classes in a Greek city, where there was no real aristocracy, no class ennobled by the public services or the abilities of their ancestors, and preserving a certain tradition of nobility—for such a class had almost wholly perished from the "progressive" Greek cities. They are audacious, obstinately self-willed; they have no respect for authorities[2] in their ribald talk, where even angels would shrink from expressing a defamatory opinion if they were bringing a charge before God. They pride themselves on living the free life of nature, like the wild beasts, ignorant of moral law and restraint, born to perish. And they shall perish.[3]

13b: Finding their pleasure in luxurious reveling during the day,[4] blots upon life,[5] indulging in luxury at their love feasts (*agape*) as they revel in your company, the vicious soul gleaming in their eyes: they bring into Christian rites the pagan license (1 Cor. 11:21–22).[6]

15: They have forsaken the right path and have gone astray, following the path of Balaam, who loved the pay of wrongdoing though even the ass corrected him. (The allusion to Balaam, bribed to teach vice and luxury to the Israelites, has become stereotyped.)

17: They are untrustworthy; they merely cheat the dupes among the young converts, whom they mislead with their boastful, self-confident language, promising them liberty while they are themselves slaves to their vices.

It seems beyond question that this description is drawn from the same class of persons who are alluded to in the messages to Pergamum and Thyatira, and whose action in Corinth prompted Paul's allusions in 8:10 and 11:22, and produced the evils at the *agape* which he denounces in 11:20ff. The method of treatment of the subject has been fixed by Paul; the temptations of Israel are taken as typical of the temptations that beset the new Christians. Balaam (as he is described in Numbers 31:16 and Josephus, *Antiquities* 4:104ff) gave the advice to tempt the Hebrews by means of the Midianite women. A mere allusion to "the way of Balaam" in 2 Peter 1:15 and "the error of Balaam" in Jude 11 is sufficient to recall the familiar illustration. In both those places the allusion is evidently a current and stereotyped formula.

In Revelation 2:14 the allusion is introduced with greater appearance of originality and is fully explained. But one cannot, from that single case, argue that Revelation 2 is earlier than 2 Peter 2; for it lies in the nature of all moral exhortations sometimes to state in explanatory detail a traditional type. On the whole the tone of the messages to Pergamum and Thyatira in Revelation 2 perhaps suggests a more developed stage than 2 Peter 2, after that special temptation or tendency had become a recognized form of thought and life, but still within the church.

We observe a steadily growing body of accepted principles. The judgments of Paul are assumed as fundamental by the authors of 2 Peter and Revelation. A question that has come before him and been decided is not permitted to come up again for discussion. What has been permitted by him is a part of ordinary Christian life.

What has been denounced by him becomes a curse to those who practice it; and the teachers who permit it are teachers of falsehood for whom destruction is gaping.

It is true that a distinct difference of spirit is perceptible between the attitude of St. Paul and that of St. John towards the Roman state. The former does not despair of, in fact he hopes for and strives after, peaceful development of the church under the protection which the existing government gives to all orderly and contented citizens. "The Christians should avoid, so far as is consistent with religion, the appearance of interfering with the present social order: the proper rule of life is to accept the world's facts, not as in themselves right, but as indifferent, and to waste no time and thought on them."[7] Only religious duty must not be violated, that is, there must be no complicity with idolatry.

On the other hand, John has become convinced of "the absolute and irreconcilable opposition between the church and the empire": he has "no thought of the possibility of bringing the state to a milder policy by convincing it of the harmlessness of Christianity."[8]

But in the same pages where that difference was pointed out it was also shown that the change of spirit was due, not to any real difference in the principles of the Christian leaders, but to the change of policy on the part of the state. Paul wrote while the early policy of Nero, that is, the policy of Seneca, guided the action of the government. John wrote after that policy had been abandoned, and the government had resolved to regard all Christians as outlaws and enemies.

We now see that Paul, even while he was instructing his converts to respect, so far as possible, the existing facts of society, was as firmly persuaded as John that the Christians must keep themselves apart from the present fabric of society. There was no possible place for them in the most characteristic and universal social institutions. The necessary inference was that these must all be destroyed, and society must be reestablished on a Christian basis.

Paul was neither bigoted nor intolerant. He appreciated the value of education. "He advised his pupils to learn from the surrounding world everything that was worthy in it."[9] He did not think that they must go out of the world; they may and should continue in the world (1 Cor. 5:10). But his opinion was unhesitating that pagan society was so leavened and impregnated by idolatry that it must be broken up before it could be reconstituted in a form reconcilable with Christian principles. Christians may remain in the world, use its teaching, profit by its opportunities. But they must not be of the world, as a part of its society.

The more closely we scrutinize the words and acts of the leading apostles, the more clearly does their perfect harmony in all essential points appear—amid some slight and purely superficial differences—and the better do we understand what is implied in Galatians 2:2, 9. Paul laid before James, Cephas, and John the gospel for the Gentiles, and they perceived the grace that was given him and gave him the right hand of fellowship. This implies that they were all from the beginning in complete agreement as to what should be the position of the Gentiles in the church and in the state.

38

The Eucharist in St. Paul's Gospel

We cannot fail to observe the extreme importance attached to the sacrament in this letter. It is the leading thought rising to the writer's lips and pen time after time in the most diverse surroundings (5:7–8; 6:17;[1] 10:16–21; 11:20–34).

It is sometimes said that the unusual number of these references is due to the fact that the epistle was written at the time of the Passover; and an argument for dating the composition has been sought from this. We cannot, however, accept this explanation. We are unable to admit that the process and evolution of thought in the letter was determined by such an accidental coincidence. In the sacrament Paul saw the antidote which the Corinthians needed to the great evil; and the greatness of the danger leads him to dwell on the antidote.

Moreover, this argument as to the date has no force unless the Christian sacrament was in that age confined to the time of Passover, which we cannot admit and which very few are likely now to maintain. The sacrament might be suggested to Paul at any season of the year, for it clearly was frequently celebrated. In 5:7–8 the Passover is mentioned (though not in such a way as to imply that it was occurring when Paul wrote). In the other places only the sacrament, not the Passover, is referred to.

Must we not infer from the epistle that special importance was attached by Paul to that rite in the building up of a church in a pagan city and in the pagan world? It was to him not merely a symbolic action. The sacrament was a real force, exerting a strong influence over the will and nature of those who shared in it. It was the one power which might counteract the constraining force of the pagan fellowships, which, as he saw, were a dangerous allurement to the leading men in the Corinthian congregation.

It was more difficult to rouse in the mind of the pagans a strong feeling of Christian brotherhood and unity than among the Jews. In the latter the feeling already existed in virtue of their own religion, which united them together and separated them from the rest of the world by its character and by its common Passover. Among the Jews all that was needed was to modify the direction of that strong feeling which they already had. But among the pagans there was no such feeling. It was strange to them, except in regard to their clubs; and therefore the Christians would find the religious unity of the club a dangerous antagonist to the proper realizing of the church unity and brotherhood.

From 5:7–8 it seems an unavoidable inference that St. Paul conceived the death of Christ to be the Paschal sacrifice: "Our Passover also has been sacrificed, Christ." The common cup and bread constitute the pledging of the participating brotherhood to their fellowship in virtue of their common relation to the sacrifice of Christ. The power of the Savior is imparted to them in the sacrament; and they become a brotherhood and a fellowship in virtue of their common relation to him: "The cup of Christ's blessing over which we bless God, does it not constitute a fellowship of the blood of Christ?"

It lies entirely outside of our purpose and province to seek to investigate the philosophic and theological ideas involved in St. Paul's conception, or to touch on later theories as to the meaning of the rite. We are satisfied to recognize that he considered that a certain force and power to move the minds and nature of the participants was communicated in the sacrament. But it is part of our task to investigate the historical origin of St. Paul's conception. That, however, must be left for a new chapter.

39

The Epistle and its Parts

As we have seen, Paul in this epistle often recurs to a former topic after an interposed discussion of another topic. Thus, in order to understand chapter 8, we have had to discuss chapter 10 along with it, so closely are they connected. Chapter 9 rises out of chapter 7. The Eucharist is the topic in 10:14–22 and 11:17–34. This characteristic is so marked that we must seek some explanation; and we shall find it in the way in which the letter was written.

It is obvious that this letter was not composed continuously at a sitting (and the same remark applies to 2 Corinthians). It is much too long for that; and, moreover, as we read it and compare it with the epistle to the Galatians, we feel that whereas the Galatian letter was thrown forth, as it were, in one single effort from the volcano of his mind, this letter to the Corinthians was written in a succession of shorter efforts, separated by intervals of thought and meditation.[1] Thus the same topic is taken up again after an interval, when reflection showed Paul that he had not exhausted what ought to be said about it.

In observing the nature of these intervals and the signs of them in the thought and style, we must, of course, bear in mind the nature of the document. It is not a treatise where continuity of style is a law of the work. It is a letter where frank, unfettered utterance of the momentary tone of mind and spirit is right. A letter ceases to be a letter if the laws of correct style that govern a formal treatise are applied to it. The perfect naturalness and spontaneity of Paul's letters is among their most marked characteristics. The thoughts in his mind seem to crystallize in words, almost unbidden, according to the mood of the moment: pleasure, grief, thankfulness, horror, and gratitude mold the style by turns.

When we speak of intervals, we need not, of course, maintain that these are necessarily always intervals of time. Sometimes they may only be changes of emotion; but doubtless they often corresponded to breaks of time. On the other hand, we need not maintain that Galatians was written in an absolutely unbroken sweep of emotion, and we may be quite certain that the vehemence of emotion prevented any noticeable interval of time from intervening between the beginning and the end.

We shall, therefore, speak of the intervals between the parts of the Corinthian epistle without insisting that they all necessarily imply appreciably long lapses of time. But some of them, at any rate, correspond to real intervals of time, during which much thought and meditation occurred. And also we may be quite confident that the composition of this epistle lasted over some considerable number of weeks, possibly some months. We cannot suppose that Paul withdrew himself for a time from his work in Ephesus in order to devote himself entirely to Corinth. His Ephesian work was heavy, continuous, exacting. He could only snatch from it short intervals for other work. Yet, at the same time, the care of Corinth lay always in his mind. Even while he was teaching and preaching in Ephesus, the thought about Corinthian needs was incubating and maturing in his heart. But the epistle was composed by parts—not in one volcanic eruption like Galatians—and it was dictated in parts, so that certain topics were treated, set aside, and recalled again for completion, as we see in the epistle which lies before us.

We do not mean that, whenever any thought recurs after the lapse of a certain number of verses or chapters, one of those intervals (as they have been defined in the last two or three paragraphs) must have intervened between the two occurrences of the thought. On the contrary, there are what we have already described as dominant thoughts, which tend constantly to recur. Those dominant thoughts spring out of the most pressing dangers to which the Corinthians were exposed. Such, for example, was idolatry, with the inevitable low standard of life and thought connected with it.[2] The pressure of pagan surroundings and pagan habits was a continuous force tending to lower the Corinthian standard of conduct; it allied itself with everything else that was hostile to truth. Therefore the thought of this danger recurs in the epistle very often, and is sometimes latent even where it is not clearly expressed.

We must then think of the epistle to the Corinthians as lying for some considerable period beside Paul, and receiving additions from time to time before it was sent away. It may be regarded as rather a series of letters than a single letter, though it was sent to Corinth as one. Its parts sprang separately from his mind, as the thoughts of his anxious and provident spirit demanded instant expression.

The proof of this view lies in the demonstration of the parts and of their significance when regarded separately. This is contained in the following sections, in which particularly the formal proof is given that an interval of time occurred between the first and the second part.

But, first, the question arises why he did not send away each part as it was written. If his care for Corinth forced him to write a few pages, would it not also force him to send off the letter immediately, that the remedy might be applied as quickly as possible? We must, for example, think that the Galatian letter, when written, was dispatched immediately. We cannot imagine Paul waiting a day needlessly after writing it. Some parts of the Corinthian letter are also extremely urgent and impassioned. Why should they be written and laid aside for weeks before being sent away?

The circumstances of Pauline epistolography furnish a ready explanation.

40

Letter Writing in Ephesus

Several excellent contributions have been made in recent years to the better understanding of the New Testament epistles through a comparison with the ordinary epistolary customs of the time. The writings of Professor Adolf Deissmann and Professor Rendel Harris deserve special recognition in this respect. We shall try to build on their foundation.

The want of a regular postal service seems to have exerted some influence on both the epistles to the Corinthians. Letters could not be sent to a distance, except when the writer found some chance of safe conveyance. As to the frequency of such opportunities, we are apt to get an erroneous impression from Cicero's correspondence—especially with Atticus, which was sometimes carried on by daily letters. Atticus, as a great businessman and financier engaged in large provincial operations requiring constant communication, had at his command a considerable body of regular letter-bearers, *tabellarii*. Cicero also maintained a large establishment of slaves. When they were resident in different parts of central Italy, they could easily keep up a daily system of messengers. Moreover, Cicero from his high position could often avail himself of the public couriers, who were constantly going back and forward on government service. And he seems to have done so a good deal, as for example, when he was in his Cilician province.

Paul was in an entirely different position. He had no slaves in Ephesus to act as letter carriers. Moreover, it is highly probable that he never entrusted his letters to any but confidential messengers—Christians—often his own subordinates and coadjutors in mission work, who could supplement the letter by verbal instructions, and might bring back to Paul reports of what they had seen. In the winter and spring of A.D. 55–56,[1] within which period 1 Corinthians must have been written, not many opportunities can have presented themselves for sending letters to Corinth from Ephesus. The season was unfavorable to direct voyages across the open sea, where the rocky Aegean islands offered few harbors and generally dangerous coasts. It is not to be understood that the direct passage between Corinth and Ephesus was entirely closed during the winter season. The Greeks were not such timid sailors as that would imply. But regular communication and ordinary trade were broken off, though undoubtedly some government vessels and occasional trading vessels watched a favorable wind and ran across. In the scarcity of vessels offering a passage—for government vessels would not be at his service—and the rarity of suitable messengers, Paul might have to wait a long time in the winter for an opportunity of sending a letter.

Now how are we to conceive Paul to have acted? Would he wait until a suitable messenger was found ready to start, and then write a letter to be sent off with him the moment it was written? Such is apparently the general view, for the date when this epistle was written is discussed commonly with the tacit assumption that the composition was a matter of a few days at most. For example, many modern scholars say that it must have been written at Passover—an assertion against which we have already protested on other grounds and against which we now raise this new objection. We have seen that the composition of the letter must have lasted over a considerable time.

Paul wrote as his heart prompted, but had to wait until an opportunity occurred of sending the letter. In the meantime new thoughts demanded expression. Thus 1 Corinthians was a series of shorter letters; and soon after it was dispatched, 2 Corinthians was begun and continued in the same way.

Examples occur even in Cicero, with his abundant postal opportunities, of this kind of composite letter. In letters to his ordinary correspondents they can rarely occur, for he was not so much interested in them as to find relief in expressing his mind to them. But occasionally, in writing to Atticus, he keeps a letter beside him and adds to it as the humor prompts him.

41

Intervals and Pauses in the Epistle

The following intervals, marked by change in emotion and change in style, have come before us in the epistle, so far as we have yet proceeded.

The first four chapters have all the appearance of perfect continuity, with an unbroken sweep of emotion. It will be shown in the following sections that Paul had actually brought his letter to an end here and arranged for its transmission, when his plans were interrupted.

Chapters 5 and 6 were written immediately on receipt of some disastrous and unexpected news from Corinth. The emotion is in marked contrast with the preceding and the following chapters. The contrast is most sharply expressed in 6:5, "I say this to move you to shame," as compared with 4:14, "I do not write these things to shame you."

A feeling of horror pervades these chapters 5 and 6. In chapter 5 this feeling rises naturally out of the subject; but it continues through 6, where the first fault rebuked is rather an error of judgment than a crime; and it soon draws back the writer's thought to the repulsive side of life, on which he was dwelling in chapter 5. Throughout these two chapters those sentences which are expressed in the first person singular are sharp and imperative in tone. They are a command.

On the other hand, in chapters 7 and 8, error of judgment, lack of sympathy, and brotherliness are implied among the Corinthians; but quiet dispassionate reasoning and argument is Paul's method of treating their case. Where the first person singular comes in, it is either to mention Paul's own example and opinion, confidently reckoned on as likely to influence their minds, or it is an appeal to the universality of custom and law in the churches. It states a deliberate opinion, but rarely issues a command. Even where the subject requires that a rule be laid down, it is done in a less imperative tone than in chapters 5 and 6; and the manner quickly returns to argument and statement of opinion. The two main topics of 7 and 8 are treated in a similar spirit and end on the same note, namely, Paul's opinion and example.

Then comes a marked interval; and in 9 and 10, in a warm emotional tone, Paul takes up again the two topics which he has just treated.

The interval between chapters 5 and 6 and chapters 7 and 8 is marked as clearly in style as in emotion. In the latter, Paul seems to have begun with the intention of taking up and discussing one by one the points on which the Corinthians had consulted him. Hence the orderly method, as if he were counting them one by one on his fingers.

7:1 περὶ δὲ ὧν ἐγράψατε
8 λέγω δὲ τοῖς ἀγάμοις
10 τοῖς δὲ, γεγαμηκόσι παραγγέλλω, ούκ ἐγώ,
12 τοῖς δὲ, λοιποῖς λέγω ἐγω
25 περὶ δὲ τῶν παρθένων
8:1 περὶ δὲ τῶν εἰδωλοθύτων

Now contrast that manner with the paragraphic connection in the preceding chapters. Notice the abrupt, excited question with which chapter 6 begins—

> Dare any of you?

And the astonished expression in the opening of chapter 5—

> It is actually reported that—

It is difficult to think that the person who dictated chapters 5–6 to his secretary proceeded immediately to the sober, orderly enumeration of chapters 7 and 8. An interval of time, bringing with it greater calmness of feeling, must have occurred.

But an interval is equally well marked between chapters 8 and 9. The style changes, and the emotion becomes far more vehement. The orderly progress of the reasoning ceases, to be resumed again in chapter 12. But in chapter 9 Paul opens with a series of question, "Am I not free? Am I not an apostle?" and so on. He considers that he is being examined, that he is making his defense, and that the judges who are examining him have little right to be assuming that position (9:3); and then his defense again turns into a further series of almost indignant questions.

We notice, too, that the sequence of thought is broken by chapter 9. The views about sacrificial meats, begun in chapter 8, are not continued till we come to chapter 10; and then the subject is taken up afresh and treated in a far deeper way, and also in a more emotional tone. I cannot think that, if Paul had already had chapter 10 in his mind, he would have written chapter 8 as it is. In fact, 10:23ff. repeats in a more precise way what is already said in rather confused fashion in chapter 8.

As we notice the superior clearness of 10:23ff., we remember that chapters 7 and 8 as a whole never strike a clear and penetrating note. They lack the sure insight of the prophet and lawgiver who goes to the heart of the question. They show much good sense, taste, sympathy; but they are rather uncertain in their treatment, and leave a blurred image on the reader's mind. It is as if Paul had begun to answer the Corinthian questions before he had fully thought out the situation, and then, leaving off for a time, had returned in chapters 9–10 to the same topics, with a clearer conception of the Corinthian intention in putting the questions.

That is most patent as we compare chapter 10 with chapter 8. Some may think that chapter 9 does not stand in a similar relation to 7. But our view is that, even here, the same relation holds good, though it is less clear. As Paul thought over the Corinthians' questions, he became more clearly conscious that their suggested cure for society, namely, the urging of marriage as a duty on all Christians, was personal to himself, making the first stage, which must culminate in open questioning of his authority over them and his apostolic rights. Hence arises the personal character of chapter 9. An emphatic statement of his authoritative position toward the Corinthians was necessary.

The strength and personality[1] of Paul's repeated claims to authority in this epistle and his repeated injunctions that the Corinthians should imitate him may easily offend the modern reader. In truth, it needs some effort before one can reconcile them with the ordinary humility, candor, and freedom from egotism or self-assertion of Paul's character. They give the occasion for the accusation which some scholars make against him, that he was excitable, irritable under opposition, unable to endure any difference of opinion or independence of judgment in those with whom he was brought into relation, surrounding himself with creatures of moderate abilities, who would obey him without questioning and follow him without murmur.[2]

The reason and the need for the assertiveness of this epistle lies in that failing of the Corinthian character (and of the Greeks generally), which we have often had to mention—their incapacity to obey and their weakness in recognizing and acting on general, moral, and legal principles. We have pointed out why Paul could not counsel the Corinthians to obey their constituted officials; but repeatedly he impresses on them the duty of obedience to their spiritual father. He felt strongly that this was a prime necessity in the present state of the Corinthian church. And in urging it on them he is unconscious of the seeming egotism. That appearance of egotism was a minor consideration; and Paul always sacrificed all minor aims in the effort to attain the great end. On this subject, see further in chapter 43.

Yet he gives a full explanation of this apparent egotism. They are to obey and imitate him, not for himself. He came to them not trusting in eloquence or in philosophy, but in the power of God, which spoke through him (2:1, 4–5). Personally, he had been weak, anxious, fearful. But they can safely follow implicitly what he said, and imitate what he did, because it was not his own power and skill that spoke to them.

The frequent repetition of the order "to imitate me" implies that it was much needed. This may seem inconsistent with the emphatic declaration in 11:2, "I praise you that you remember me in all things, and hold fast the traditions, even as I delivered them unto you." But it has been rightly recognized[3] that this really contains a quotation from the Corinthians' letter to himself: it means, "I am glad to hear from you that you remember me in all things."

42

The First Letter Contained in First Corinthians

As we have seen, the first four chapters of the epistle are written in one sustained, continuous tone and emotion. They were dictated at one time—or, at least, at very brief intervals—under the influence of the same overmastering thought and purpose, and form as perfect a unity as the Galatian epistle. They come to a distinct climax and conclusion. The paragraph 4:14–21 reviews and sums up the purpose of the short letter in a pointed, emphatic way—as was Paul's custom—and states his intentions for the future. He is sending Timothy at the present moment. Soon he will himself come. They should so act, as not to need rebuke when he reaches them. At this point the final greetings, which commonly lead up to the benediction, might come in with perfect propriety.

We have in these chapters a perfect little letter, a model of a religious and hortatory, warning and friendly epistle.

The occasion of that letter was evidently the news received from the agents of Chloe (1:2; see chapter 9). It is filled with the thought that the Corinthian Christians are spending their time and energy in discussing the merits of rival preachers, backing their favorites in the true Greek spirit (see chapter 5), and thus tending to fall into rival parties wearing, as it were, the badges of their respective favorites. It explains his method of teaching, stage by stage, according to the progress of his pupils.

At the same time, the letter speaks not for himself alone, but for all the apostles. All are agreed; all stand or fall together. To balance one against another is to miss utterly the true and perfect unity that reigns among them all. Their other teachers and favorites also adapt their teaching to the stage at which they find their pupils. But all are aiming at the same result: all would try to prevent the

Corinthians from this folly of pitting one teacher against the other (4:6).

The remedy lies in faithfulness to the first and effectual teaching, through which they had been converted.

43

The Single Standard and the Monarchical Bishop

The stress which Paul lays on the necessity of a single standard for the congregation deserves special note. Many teachers have come, and many will come, for one teacher at the beginning was not sufficient. But not all are to be trusted. There must, therefore, be some standard by which to test them.

That standard should be sought in the original teaching, namely, the teaching of the founder of the congregation. His teaching was the true, divine message; for it came in power (2:4–5; 4:20; 9:2). The existence of a church in Corinth is the proof that Paul's message was the right and the standard teaching. Paul had laid the foundation, "which is Christ" (3:10–11).

Other teachers do well when they try to build on that foundation; but their superstructure will be tried and tested by fire, whether it is vital and true. The proof of their teaching will be the same as the proof of Paul's. The power to last is the ultimate test.

In 3:11–15 Paul is saying anew what he said to the Galatians (Gal. 1:6–9): "If anyone else, if even I myself, should preach unto you any other gospel than that which I and Barnabas preached unto you, let him be *anathema*." But in that place Paul was looking from the opposite point of view. He was thinking of teachers who were building on his foundation a building inconsistent therewith. Here he is thinking of teachers who are building on his foundation what is in harmony therewith.

But the congregation needs to try the new teachers at the present moment; and it finds a standard in the first teaching, which has proved itself to be vital and enduring. The congregation itself is the living proof that the first teaching was true; and it must reject all that does not agree with that standard. To the Galatians and the

Corinthians alike that is the principle which Paul urges. Even if he himself came giving a second and different message, they must reject him. His first, effectual message is the only true one.

Their standard, then, must be single. They must look to one guide alone; and that guide is their father. Many teachers will come to them; many servants will keep watch over them in their childhood:[1] but they can have only one father, Paul himself. Him they should look to and imitate.

Looking to the creative sense, the feeling for precedent in law and organization, which are evident in the growth of the early church, we can hardly hesitate to say that here we have the germinating idea out of which grew the monarchical bishops of the following century.

The difficulty was how this principle should be carried out after the apostles had passed away. Paul was succeeded by the author of First Peter, and he by the author of Revelation 1–3. But who should succeed later? Elsewhere I have attempted[2] to show the external causes under pressure of which one of the *episkopoi* or *presbyteroi* was obliged to become a president and representative of the congregation. That president-*episkopos* was, among other things, charged with the duty of communicating with other congregations, with which is closely connected the duty of entertaining visitors and messengers from other congregations. Now from the beginning the idea is clearly discernible that the general opinion of the whole church is divine and right. Obviously, the person in each congregation who could best learn what the church as a whole thought was the official charged with communication. He was the link connecting the congregation with other congregations: the sum of the scattered congregations, separated in space, makes up the church universal. The letters, visits, and other communications are the device whereby space is annihilated, and unity attained. Thus communication between the scattered parts was the life of the church, and the official charged with communication was obviously presented as the heir to the authority of the apostles. So far the argument has been already stated; but we ask when and how this development was first recognized as a necessity.

Paul undoubtedly had the idea that the single authority, necessary for his churches, must not perish with himself. In his first letter to Timothy there is latent the idea that Timothy is his delegate and representative in Asia. From the idea of delegation to that of succession the development is natural and necessary. How far Paul had foreseen that development we are denied any information. But, in fact, it seems beyond doubt that the president-*episkopos* became the heir to the monarchical authority; and all reasonable probability is in favor of that inheritance having been contemplated by some of the apostles themselves.

The third epistle of John takes us into the time before that inheritance was settled. It is addressed to Gaius, who was evidently charged with the duties of hospitality in his own congregation (5:5). His congregation was situated on one of the great lines of communication along which Christianity spread towards the Gentiles.[3] To his care Demetrius is recommended in this letter of introduction. But a certain Diotrephes discourages and opposes that welcoming of visitors from other congregations, which Gaius extends to them; and he also resists the authority of the writer, who evidently claims the same general authority which Paul and Peter had exercised. Diotrephes, who "casts them out of the church," is evidently understood to be an official; and the situation implied is one of division and contention between rival influences in a congregation, such as showed the urgent need of a single standard of authority in it. He was one of those "headstrong and self-willed persons" who "kindled sedition" in Corinth (1 Clement 1.1) and beyond doubt in many other congregations.

44

Plans for a Second Visit to Corinth

The fact that the composition of the epistle extended over a considerable period affords a complete explanation of the variation between Paul's statements about his second visit to Corinth; and at the same time, a comparison between his different statements proves conclusively that one of the intervals in the composition of 1 Corinthians must lie between chapter 4 and chapter 5.

When Paul wrote the concluding paragraph of this short letter (4:14–21), he was sending Timothy to Corinth and intending to come himself shortly. Verse 17: "For this cause I have sent[1] unto you Timothy, who shall put you in remembrance of my ways"; verse 19: "But I will come to you shortly, if the Lord wills." Now if we compare this passage with the similar ones in Philippians 2:25, Colossians 4:7–9, and Ephesians 6:21, it becomes clear that Timothy is here commissioned as a special envoy to Corinth. The four passages correspond exactly to one another. Timothy is to go direct from Ephesus to Corinth, carrying instructions and a letter. Epaphroditus is sent from Rome to Philippi with a letter,[2] "that when you see him again, you may rejoice." Tychicus (with Onesimus) was sent from Rome to Colossae and Ephesus bearing two letters, "that you may know our estate, and that he may comfort your hearts." The same word and tense is used in all four cases (ἔπεμψά, πέμψαι).

The parallel between 1 Corinthians 4:17–19 and Philippians 2:19–25 is even closer. In both cases Paul intimates an ulterior plan, using the same word "shortly" (ταχέως). He sends Timothy now, and will himself come shortly. He sends Epaphroditus now, and will send Timothy shortly.

But these intentions, as mentioned here, were partly frustrated, and were carried out in a different way from what is here intimated. Timothy did not go direct to Corinth; and hence Paul says in 16:10,

"If Timothy comes," in a tone of uncertainty (ἐὰν ἔλθῃ, not, εἰ ἔρχεται), which contrasts markedly with the assured "I have sent Timothy to you" of 4:17. The facts are left obscure for us in the epistle, while the march of events had made them clear to the Corinthians; but Luke explains them in Acts 19:22. Timothy was, after all, not sent directly to Corinth, but went round by way of Macedonia.

The reason for the change remains uncertain; but probably it was due, in part at least, to the winter season, and the difficulty of getting a passage direct across the open Aegean. Macedonia needed Timothy at the moment; and it was resolved that he should go there first, and afterwards, if circumstances were suitable, go on to Corinth.[3] Then Paul kept the letter which he had intended to send by Timothy, and reserved it for another opportunity and another messenger.

Nor did Paul carry out exactly his intention, here announced, of shortly going himself to Corinth. He alludes to his change of intention in 2 Corinthians 1:15ff.: "I was minded to come before unto you for a second visit to confirm you, and thereafter to visit Macedonia and return to you again, so as to be ready to start from Corinth for Jerusalem in time for the Passover of the coming year" (i.e., March 57). He apologizes for the change of plan, and explains that the change was not due to fickleness and wavering uncertainty of mind on his part, but was made in kindness to the Corinthians themselves. Paul did not wish to come to bring them sorrow. He wished to come to bring them happiness. He preferred to send a letter conveying his severity and reproofs, and to come later in more pleasant circumstances.

Surely then the reasonable interpretation of this passage must be that Paul had intended to go direct to Corinth from Ephesus, and had intimated his intention. But bad news came. He learned that the conduct of the Corinthians required severe reproof. He resolved to reprove them by letter, to postpone his visit, and to go first into Macedonia.

Such is the sequence of events, as we gather it from 2 Corinthians 1:15ff. Paul intimates his intention of soon going direct to Corinth. The visit is intimated in a kind, not in a severe tone. Paul anticipates that it will be a pleasant visit: there is not a trace of sternness or severity in the short letter in 1 Corinthians 1–4, though, of course, there is that admonition which young human converts always need—"not to shame you, but to admonish you as my beloved children" (4:14). But the tone of chapter 5 is completely changed. This new chapter is full of horror and stern rebuke. Evidently here begins the letter of severe reproof. Paul has heard the terrible news. He at once abandons all thought of an early visit to Corinth, and instead writes the letter which begins with chapter 5.

But he had still beside him the letter of chapters 1–4, which he had intended to send by Timothy, but had retained when Timothy had to go by way of Macedonia. Paul did not destroy that letter. He sent it, but first he lengthened it by adding a long and outspoken expression of his horror and astonishment at the laxity of moral feeling in the Corinthian church.

The lengthened epistle had to wait for a suitable messenger and an occasion. The visit of Stephanas and Fortunatus and Achaicus, who brought the letter form the Corinthians, probably lasted some time, as they either had come on some business purpose or took the opportunity of combining business with their duty as envoys.[4] Paul worked on the letter at intervals until some time in the spring; and in chapter 16:3–8 he states his final intention, regardless of the discrepancy with 9:19. He will wait in Ephesus till Pentecost on May 9, 56. Then he will go to Macedonia, and thereafter he will visit Corinth, whence he will either go to Jerusalem (in the spring of 57) or send envoys thither.

He makes in this epistle no explanation of, or apology for, the change of plan. Probably he, at the moment of writing, did not think of the inconsistency between 4:19 and 16:3ff. He was so absorbed in serious topics that minor discrepancies did not affect him. But soon afterwards he remembered; and as he was now beginning to compose 2 Corinthians, he apologized in the opening paragraphs for the change and the discrepancy. In the interval, however, other changes had occurred. He was unable to remain in Ephesus till Pentecost. The riot of Demetrius compelled him to retire for the time, as freedom to speak was no longer in his power. Probably he had not waited till the three messengers were ready to return to Corinth; but had sent Titus as his envoy,[5] with instructions as to how he should address the erring Corinthians and orders to bring back a report to Paul. Titus, aware that Paul was to travel from Ephesus by way of Troas and Macedonia, returned that way; and in the coasting system of ancient travel there was no danger the two should miss one another, inasmuch as each was on the outlook for the other. They met in Macedonia (2 Cor. 6: 6–7).

It seems strange that, considering the obviously close connection between the latter part of First Corinthians and the early chapters of Second Corinthians, many commentators attempt to interpose a long interval between them. It is obvious that the beginning of the second epistle was written before Titus returned, and there is every reason to think that he would not stay long in Corinth or linger on the road, considering Paul's extreme anxiety about the state of that church. The second epistle was continued after Titus met Paul and relieved his mind. The first part was evidently written in Troas,[6] the second in Macedonia (probably Philippi).

It is remarkable how many erroneous statements have been made by modern scholars about this simple matter—all due to the inveterate habit (a legacy from the Tübingen School) of beginning by framing an ingenious and tempting theory, and then squeezing Paul's words to suit it.

For example, one writer[7] infers rightly from 2 Corinthians 2:3 that Paul had written to the Corinthians that he was coming to them, and proceeds, "he did not write this in any extant letter. In the first epistle he still declared categorically that he would come. It can only be inferred that he wrote it in a letter subsequent to the first epistle, and that must have been the letter carried by Titus." This argument fails to catch the point of Paul's statements. The contradictory intentions which Paul in 2 Corinthians 1:2 implies that he had intimated to the Corinthians were not "I will come to you" and "I will not come to you"; they were "I will come direct to you before I go to Macedonia" and "I will go to Macedonia first, postponing you to a later time." Both these intentions are intimated in the first epistle (4:17 and 16:5); and the direct contradiction between them is not there explained or apologized for. Thus, as Paul feels, he has sent the Corinthians a word (i.e., a letter) that is at once "Yea" and "Nay;" and he apologizes and explains.

It would, however, be endless to go over all the difficulties that have been needlessly and unjustifiably invented, and the incorrect inferences that have been drawn from the passages bearing on Paul's intended and postponed visit. One alone must be briefly noticed, inasmuch as it is especially unreasonable, namely, the theory which would place the composition of the latter chapters of the second epistle before the early chapters. It is clear that in 2 Corinthians 1:15 Paul explains why he had not paid a second visit to Corinth as he had once intended, and that in 2 Corinthians 12:14 and 13:1, he is looking back over two visits and forward to a third. The full explanation of this difference must be left to the commentary on the second epistle. But, at least, the difference proves clearly that the final chapter of the second epistle was written later than the opening chapter.

45

The Apostolate

Nowhere does Paul state in clearer terms his views about the authority vested in an apostle, and about the origin of that office, than in the chapter which we now approach. His own authority in Corinth was questioned, and he justifies it. Let us first try to understand exactly[1] what he says, and then determine what can be fairly inferred.

9:1. "Am I not an apostle," that is, an accredited envoy and representative of Christ, dispatched into the world? Am I not independent of any control exercised by any human power? Have I not come into direct and immediate relations with Christ, by being permitted to see Him and thus enabled to bear witness to the world of His glorified state? Is not my right made evident to all by your existence as a church in Corinth?

2. Even if I should not be recognized as an apostle elsewhere, yet assuredly I am an apostle so far as you are concerned; for you are the seal guaranteeing the genuineness of my apostolic powers.

3. This is my answer to such as inquire into my rights and my position.[2] The authority which Paul claims in Corinth is based on his position as the apostle or envoy sent to them. If a proof is sought that his apostolate is genuine, it is found in his success: the Corinthian church is his proof. Such always is the ultimate test, as he has previously stated (see chapter 43). As an apostle, he is free; that is, he is independent of all human control. No person or persons have any right to order or limit his action; he does, or refrains from doing, according to his own judgment of what his apostolate requires.

But whence does his commission as an apostle originate? How has he been appointed? In reply to that question he appeals to the fact that he has seen Jesus. The importance of this seeing of Jesus leads Paul to insist on it at greater length elsewhere in writing to the Corinthians. That is one of the leading ideas in the epistles: it was one that rose again and again in his mind as a fact of special importance for them. He insists on it in no other of his letters; but to the Corinthians he mentions it in 9:1, 15:8, and 2 Corinthians 12:3–4.[3] The reason for this insistence lies in the necessity of bringing home to them his apostolic commission. His glory and his peculiar honor was that he had been admitted more than once to come into direct relations with Jesus, and so marked out as His envoy and apostle. He was one of the witnesses that Jesus was living.

Thus the argument comes practically to the same issue as we have seen in Galatians:[4] the only parties to be considered are the converted, the messenger, and the divine author of the message. No human authority can for a moment claim to intrude between these three.

Considering how important, how absolutely fundamental for Paul it is that his commission originates directly from God, and that no human power intervenes so as to acquire any authority over him, we cannot understand the opinion expressed by some distinguished scholars, whom we would gladly follow to the utmost possible limit, that he (and so too Barnabas) was not actually constituted an apostle until he was invested with that office by the church in Antioch (Acts 13:2). There is something hid from us, or alien to us, in the process by which such an opinion is reached.[5]

46

"Am I Not Free?" (9:1)

That the meaning of "free" here is as we have assumed in the preceding section seems clearly proved by 9:19: "though I be free from all, yet have I made myself a servant[1] unto all." I have allowed my acts to be guided and determined by men, accommodating myself to them, in order to gain more complete success. The antithesis is rather rhetorical; but all its force comes from the sense which we have given to the word "free."

It is characteristic of Paul's tone to the Corinthians that, while he claims freedom as a right, he says that in practice he has made himself a servant, a slave. In this epistle he glorifies the duty of obedience and voluntary servitude. To the Galatians, on the contrary, he glorifies freedom. The difference in this respect between the two epistles is very striking; and it shows how necessary it is always to interpret Paul's words by reference to the character and circumstances of his audience. The slavish Phrygians are called to freedom (5:13): that is the divine gift to them (5:1). The Jerusalem which is now lies in bondage, but freedom belongs to the Jerusalem which is above (4:26). The Galatians are born free as the sons of the free woman and not of the slave mother (4:31).

On the other hand, the Corinthians, too self-confident and too little disposed to obedience, are often reminded that freedom is not to be sought as an end always in itself desirable.[2] A mere numerical statement sufficiently indicates the difference of tone: the words "free" and "freedom" occur 10 times in the 6 chapters of Galatians, 7 times in the 16 chapters of 1 Corinthians, and once in the 13 chapters of 2 Corinthians.[3] But when we look at the spirit of the passages in which "freedom" is mentioned to the Corinthians, the contrast to Galatians becomes still more marked. In 9:1 Paul insists on his freedom, but he adds in 9:19 that he has voluntarily made himself a slave. He points out that in the church the slave has equal advantages with the free man (12:13),[4] and should not set it before himself as an object to attain freedom (7:21).[5] Freedom of conscience may be a danger to others (10:29).

It is quite wrong to think, as some do, that Paul found he had gone too far in Galatians in praising freedom; and in Corinthians corrected his teaching so as to praise obedience. The advice in each case is relative to the audience. In each case Paul sees and says that freedom is the highest condition, though there are dangers in seeking after it too hastily. But in the one case it is prudent to insist more on the dangers, in the other on the advantages of freedom.

While Paul sees that it is necessary to impress strongly on the Corinthians the duty of obedience, we observe in what a generous and lofty way he does this. There is nowhere any expression that might tend to break the spirit or wound the just self-respect of the Corinthians. No better example could be quoted of true nobility of mind than the manner in which Paul counsels them to be content with less than absolute freedom, and to acquiesce in the control of wisdom and authority.

47

Privileges of an Apostle

In Chapter 9 Paul mentions several privileges of an apostle.
9:4. Have we not privilege to be maintained, while resident among you, at the cost of the church? You know that we have.
5. Have we not privilege to take about with us a Christian woman for wife, as also the rest of the apostles, and the brethren of the Lord, and Cephas?[1]
6. Or is it only I and Barnabas that have not privilege to abstain from working for our bread?
7. The soldier is maintained by the state. The tenant (*métayer*) who plants the vineyard (though he is not the owner of the soil and the vines, but merely contributes the work and divides with the owner the profits), eats the fruit of it (i.e., not to consume it all, but he is free to use the fruit for his own personal needs). He who tends a flock for the owner uses the milk for his own needs.

Three illustrations are here taken from common life.[2] The soldier is fed by the state: the illustration is drawn rather from the standing army of the Romans than the citizen force of a Greek city: it is more Roman than Greek.[3] The agricultural system of *métayers* working the soil and paying a proportion of the crops to the owner was widespread under various modifications in ancient times.

This paragraph, with the following, has no bearing on the argument, unless the Corinthians had been struck by a contrast between Paul and some other teacher or teachers who lived at the expense of the community. Nor would it be sufficient to suppose that the Corinthians had heard that teachers in other places were supported by the congregation. Something that had come home to them in Corinth is needed to make the situation and the words intelligible. Apollos had gone to Corinth after Paul; but his conduct alone would not explain the prominence given here to the action of the apostles. Something further must have occurred; and the thought of this, and of the talk roused in Corinth by it, is in Paul's mind. This event can hardly have been anything else than the appearance in Corinth of some important personage who took advantage of the privileges which Paul denied himself.

48

St. Peter in Corinth

One of the most striking facts in this first Corinthian epistle is the prominent position which St. Peter occupies in it.

1. A group or class of Christians in Corinth hold by him: "I am (a partisan) of Cephas" was their motto. It is implied in 1:12 and 3:22 that the Corinthians discussed the merits and style of Paul and Apollos and Cephas as teachers, and some preferred the one, some another, while others again were not content with the exposition of Christ as given by any of them (see chapter 5).

2. In the passage before us Peter is singled out, separated from "the rest of the apostles," and used to mark a climax rising from them, through "the brethren of the Lord" to "Cephas." This peculiar prominence is assigned to him in respect of a personal fact, namely, that he traveled accompanied by his wife and taking certain allowances.

There seems to be only two possible explanations of the importance thus attached to him. Either he was already recognized in Corinth as the supreme apostle, whose example far outweighed that of all others, or he was personally known in Corinth, so that his example was peculiarly impressive to them.

It seems impossible to hesitate for a moment between these alternatives. Not a scrap of evidence is known to support the first. The second alone can stand. People in Corinth discussed Peter's teaching and his style and his conduct—with all the free criticism that Greeks used—because they had seen him and listened to him. For the same reason they knew that he traveled in a different way from Paul.

3. He is quoted first and separately from the other apostles as a witness that Christ was still living (see 15:5). This might be sufficiently justified on chronological grounds. Luke 24:34 mentions that Christ was seen by Peter alone before he was seen by the twelve.

But his evidence would be all the weightier to the Corinthians if they had heard him tell the story himself.

Elsewhere[1] we have studied the variation in the way in which Paul mentions individuals, according as they are or are not personally known to his correspondents. When the effect of the reference to an individual depends mainly on facts not stated in the context, but presupposed as familiar to the readers, that individual is probably known personally to them. On that principle we infer that Chloe and Sosthenes and Apollos were personally known in Corinth, and so also Cephas.

Nor is there anything improbable or strange in this conclusion. The Corinthian tradition was that the same two apostles who preached in Rome had preached in their city—Paul and Peter. Dionysius, bishop of Corinth, mentions that fact in a letter written about A.D.170–75. A tradition, so early on such a matter, has strong claim to be considered authoritative; and J. B. Lightfoot draws the proper inference[2] from a comparison between Dionysius' statement and 1 Corinthians 1:12 and 3:22. It must then be regarded as a fact, and a very important fact, that St. Peter had preached in Corinth before this first epistle was written.

Now there is every probability—at least for those to whom the evidence seems conclusive as to St. Peter having preached in Rome—that he visited Corinth on his way to Rome. Corinth was the halfway resting-place between Syria and Rome; and it seems improbable that Peter would stop short at Corinth when we consider what is likely to have been his business on this journey.

We shall probably not be wrong in supposing that Peter's visits to Rome, to Syrian Antioch (Gal. 2:11), and to Samaria (Acts 8:14) are to be all classed together as made on behalf of the supreme church authorities. He was commissioned from Jerusalem to inspect these new churches, and to report upon them after forming an opinion as to their character. Whether he was similarly commissioned to a purely Pauline foundation like the Corinthian church is perhaps more doubtful; but we think it highly probable that he was so commissioned, for we see no reason to think that either Paul or the leading apostles in Jerusalem wished to make any distinction between his churches and the rest.

In Rome, at any rate, the young church must have been an object of much interest in Jerusalem; and those who think it unlikely that Peter would intrude on the Pauline church at Corinth as a commissioner with authority from the central body in Jerusalem must feel all the more strongly that he would be there only because it was on the way to some place beyond; and the only place beyond that has a moment's claim to consideration is Rome.

Even we who think that Peter was an authoritative commissioner in Corinth must feel that the interest attaching to the church in Rome was likely to attract him thither, and that a commission to inspect the new churches was most unlikely to stop short at Corinth.

Further, we must probably regard this visit of St. Peter as having formed part of a regular tour of inspection. "As Peter went through all parts he came also the saints which dwelt at" Derbe and Lystra and Iconium and the cities of Asia and Corinth (Acts 9:32). We must assume that he took the land route so as to visit the new churches. Moreover, if he was on his way to Rome (as we think highly probable), it would follow that he must have chosen the land route, for the sea route would not bring him to Corinth, but to Puteoli.[3] If he came to Corinth by the land route over Asia Minor, it is beyond doubt or question that he must have passed through Ephesus on the way. The regular voyage over the Aegean was between Ephesus and Corinth.

The character of this tour may perhaps explain why a staunch Paulinist like Luke did not mention it. He did not regard an inspection authorized by the church in Jerusalem as an event of importance in the development of the Pauline churches; and his rule is to mention only the great critical steps in the growth of the church.

It is an interesting point that Peter is here implied to have been accompanied by his wife when he visited Corinth. Tradition records also that she was with him in Rome and that he saw her led to martyrdom there.

49

The Date of St. Peter's Visit to Rome

It would furnish a fixed point of the highest value in an obscure subject if the precise date of St. Peter's visit to Corinth could be fixed. Apparently it had occurred some considerable time before this epistle was written, for the effects on the congregation in Corinth after his departure are alluded to in 1:11 and 3:22. Moreover, we might have looked for some more explicit allusion to the visit if it had occurred only shortly before the epistle was written (winter/spring, 55–56). Probably it was known to and mentioned by Paul in that previous letter (which is alluded to in 5:9).

The latest date for Peter's visit to Corinth, therefore, is the late spring of A.D. 55.

On the other hand it is evident from 1:12 and 3:4, 6, 22 that Apollos visited Corinth before Peter. Apollos was the first important teacher who had come there after Paul to carry on Paul's work: "I planted, Apollos watered." Now Paul passed through Ephesus in March 53; and some time afterwards Apollos arrived, was brought over to the Pauline views by Priscilla and Aquila, and sent across to work in Corinth. He had preached a little in Ephesus before he departed; and we can hardly date his arrival in Corinth earlier than the end of summer 53. He was in Corinth preaching when Paul reached Ephesus about midwinter 53; and it is very unlikely that any ordinary person would cross later than October.[1] Hence we may fairly date the arrival of Apollos in Corinth about September 53, and suppose that he spent the winter of 53–54 at least, and perhaps the whole of 54, in Corinth. These considerations show that Peter went to Corinth between spring 54 and spring 55.

But we can advance still further, and establish a fair probability that the spring of 55 was the date of the visit. The visit was doubtless a short one. Its purpose was probably, as we have seen, simply inspection, and Peter was on his way to Rome.

Now the date of Peter's visit to Rome is assigned to 55 by Lactantius in *The Deaths of the Persecutors* (*De Mortibus Persecutorum*), a work written in A.D. 313–15 and of good historical value. He says that the apostles spent twenty-five years, down to the beginning of Nero's reign,[2] in laying the foundations of the church; and that Peter came to Rome when Nero was already on the throne.[3] The writer is indubitably counting from A.D. 30 as the date of the Crucifixion to 55 as the arrival in Rome.

Dr. Karl Erbes[4] would explain this date as due to a confusion with the false date 55 assigned by Eusebius for the arrival of Paul in Rome. He is convinced, just as we are, that Eusebius made a blunder of five years in interpreting that Pauline date. But his theory that Lactantius (writing earlier than Eusebius) erred in the same way about the Pauline date and then transferred it to Peter is a very thin-spun hypothesis, such as some writers take for chronological reasoning.

We hold that Lactantius goes back to a good Roman tradition, fixing the arrival of St. Peter in the summer of 55; and the late *Liber Pontificalis* (as Dr. Erbes says) gives the same year, "Peter entered Rome in the first consulship of Nero Caesar."[5] That the whole history of Peter in Rome has been confused and distorted by the false idea that the two apostles were martyred on the same day is quite true; but the date 55 has the look of a real fragment of history, preserved in the Roman tradition.

50

Had Paul Seen Jesus? (9:1)

It is remarkable that Paul, here and in 15:8, lays such stress on his having actually seen Jesus—evidently referring to the appearance of Jesus to him near Damascus—whereas two of the three accounts of that event in Acts contain no direct statement that he saw the person who spoke to him, and even suggest that he did not see.

In Acts 9:4–8 there shone a light. Paul fell on the ground, he heard a voice, he arose from the earth, he found that he was blind. In 22:7 also there shone a light. Paul fell to the ground, he heard a voice, he could not see but had to be led. Taken alone, these two accounts would certainly suggest that Paul had only heard, but had not seen, the form. Yet in 1 Corinthians he twice claims to have seen and to be a witness to the risen Jesus.

Moreover, those two accounts represent the voice as saying to Paul, "Rise and go into the city"; and they certainly would suggest that his rising from the ground took place at the end of the vision, and was the first action resulting from it.

In Acts 26:13–20 the account varies in some important details. There shone a light, all fell to the ground, Paul heard a voice. He was ordered to rise and stand on his feet: a longer address was then made to him, declaring the intentions of Jesus in appearing to his eyes,[1] and laying stress on the fact that his work would be to bear witness of what he had seen[2] and of the circumstances in which Jesus should in future be seen by him.

We see then that the author of Acts was quite aware that Paul claimed to have seen Jesus; and when we look more closely at the other accounts, we observe that in 9:7 the men who were with him "stood speechless, hearing the voice but beholding no man." There is no point in saying that they saw nobody, unless Paul saw someone. Might we not infer from that incidental touch that Paul had seen? Yet how indirectly and briefly is the information given!

Similarly, in 22:14 Ananias reminds Paul of the vision that appeared to him, when he was chosen "to see the Righteous One, and to hear a voice from His mouth," and to be a witness of what he had seen and heard. Here again the information is given by the author, in this indirect way, through the mouth of Ananias. He knows it; but he omits in the primary narrative what is sufficiently given in the immediate sequel. He also reports in the briefest way the words addressed to Paul, omitting what seems to us to be of the greatest importance, but giving the words much more fully in another part of his book. Surely we may infer that the extreme brevity of the account in chapter 9 was compensated in the writer's plan by the fuller information which was to come in the report of Paul's speeches in chapters 22 and 26, that is, in writing chapter 9 he had before his mind chapters 22 and 26.

We see from this case how to interpret the much abbreviated narrative of the New Testament; we should never too hastily infer that, because only certain words are recorded in the account of any incident, therefore nothing else of importance was known to the writer. A detail which on some occasions St. Paul regards as of primary importance is altogether omitted both by him on one occasion, and by his friend and admirer Luke, from the account of the incident. And the omission is so made that the narrative seems to leave no gap and no room for that detail, until we find elsewhere the more complete account; and when we have that, the whole action becomes clear.

It is necessary to insist on this important principle. Most of the difficulties in early Christian history arise from failure to catch the method of the narrative.

The New Testament books have none of the character of formal treatises composed at a later time by persons who look dispassionately over past history. They bear the stamp of the stress and emotion of actual conflict. The speaker or writer remembers so vividly the details which are at the moment necessary for his immediate purpose that he leaves out or slurs quickly over other details, also important, yet not at the moment pressing on his attention.

We must also recognize the close relation between 1 Corinthians 15:1–8 and the command in Acts 22:15 and 26:16, "be a witness of what you have seen." Paul quotes to the Corinthians all the testimony which proved that Jesus was not dead: he himself is the last witness. In giving his testimony he is acting in obedience to the instruction mentioned in those two passages of Acts.

Another variation in the accounts may be noticed here. In 26:16–18 the order to preach to the Gentiles is given Paul in the vision. In

22:21 it is not given (except in the general order, "to all men" [22:15]), till long afterwards in Jerusalem. In 9:17–18 it is presumably reported by Ananias to Paul. This last account is specially remarkable. Ananias hears about Paul in a vision, receives a message to deliver to him, and is informed that Paul is chosen to preach to Gentiles and to Jews. He goes to Paul and gives him quite a different message, omitting the prophecy as to Paul's future preaching, but mentioning his vision by the way and his receiving of the Holy Spirit (neither of which is reported in Ananias' vision). It seems quite clear that the author intends us to combine what Ananias tells Paul with the account given of Ananias' vision, and to understand that all the combined details occurred in the vision, and then were all reported in full by Ananias to Paul.[3] But nothing is mentioned twice: there is no room in so abbreviated a work as the Acts for needless repetition.

But one thing comes out clear from the minute examination of the various accounts. While the commission to go to the Gentiles was given to Paul at the very beginning, it was not given in the same explicit, precise, unmistakable fashion as on a later occasion in Jerusalem (Acts 22:17ff.), shortly before the beginning of his first missionary journey. At first it was united with a commission to the Jews in 9:15 and 26:20[4] (briefly, "to all men," 22:15). Paul did not gather from the first vision a clear conception of the nature of his mission as being specially to the Gentiles. He was for a long time firmly persuaded that his experiences and his known vehemence as an enemy to the Christians qualified him specially to persuade the Jews. When at last the commission to the Gentiles was given to him in clear, brief words, he even ventured to object on the ground that the Jews knew him as the persecutor and murderer of Stephen (and therefore would believe his assurance that he has seen the living Christ).

After that definite commission Paul, in looking back to the first vision, perceived that the commission to the Gentiles was given even then, though he had not at the time recognized it.

Further, this shows probably that, in comparison to later visions, Paul's appreciation and memory of the first was more confused and blurred. That is only what must be regarded as natural. If some rare and exceptional men are so sensitive to that divine nature which surrounds us and embraces us and breathes through us as to be occasionally able, in moments of special exaltation and heightened sensibility, to commune with it, that quality in them will be strengthened during their life, and they will become more able to stand before and to comprehend the power which manifests itself to them.

Appendix

Note on the Date of Second John

A query in reference to Professor Rendel Harris's interesting note on the address of Second John in the *Expositor* for March 1901 may not be out of place here, since the forms and methods of epistolary communication are of the utmost importance in studying the Pauline letters. Professor Harris has done so much real service in this line of work that he can well afford to make allowance, if we hesitate to go with him completely. That Second John is a real letter to a lady, we entirely agree with him; and we accept his inferences as to her family and position as highly probable and almost certain.

But we cannot think that he has made out his case as to the meaning of the address—"that κύρια is a term of endearment, and should be so translated: at the least it should be 'dear lady.' " He quotes κύρια μου Σερηνία from an Egyptian letter, where Grenfell and Hunt render "my dear Serenia." But the endearment there lies in μου rather than in κυρία. Those who have been used to colloquial Greek in modern times will feel at once the difference between κυρία and κυρία μου.

The use of κύριος and κυρία in polite communication at that period seems to be exactly similar to the use of *dominus* in Latin. Professor Harris quotes another Egyptian letter, where a man addresses his own brother as κυριέ μου and concludes that "the expression must be affectionate rather than official." We remember that Seneca speaks about his brother (towards whom he had a very warm feeling) as *dominus meus Gallio* (if my memory serves me right); and we find the two cases quite parallel. But Seneca would also speak of the reigning emperor as *dominus meus* or *dominus noster*. The truth is perhaps that κύριος, κυρία, and *dominus* in the language of polite society at that time were almost colorless terms, mere forms of courtesy, and just because they were colorless in themselves they were susceptible of taking the color of the surrounding circumstances. They might be very respectful; and they might be used of one's nearest relations. But there seems to be in them no note of love or affection: that is given only through the addition of a personal pronoun. In another Egyptian letter a father writes to his son as κυρίῳ μου, but he also says δέσποτά μου, and speaks of his wife as τὴν δεσποίνην μοι. As Professor Harris himself allows, the father was "a stickler for proprieties"; and we must see elaborately polite forms in his letter.

In regard to this one detail we would ask if Professor Harris's argument might not be strengthened. But, apart from this little point, he has brought out very instructively and convincingly the early character of the epistle. In the same number we have tried to prove a similarly early date for the Third Epistle, and, as he says, it "was written at the very same time as the second."

Chapter Notes

Introduction

1. F. F. Bruce, The Acts of the Apostles (Grand Rapids: Eerdmans, 1990) xvi.

Chapter One

1. Henceforth *Galatians*; London: Hodder and Stoughton, 1899.

Chapter Two

1. *St. Paul the Traveller and the Roman Citizen* (London: Hodder and Stoughton, 1897) 260.
2. In order to show that this is not a mere random statement springing out of the attempt to illustrate the epistles, we may be permitted to add that the main thought and intention in the writer's *Impressions of Turkey* is to illustrate this principle in detail.

Chapter Four

1. *Galatians*, chapter 2.
2. Cicero, *Letters to Atticus* 9.7a.
3. Hermann Hellmuth says, "daraus schliesse ich dass Balbus der alleinige Verfasser des Briefes ist, und dass Oppius seinen Namen nur beifügte, um seine Austimmung zu dem Inhalte der Worte zu erklären" ("from that I conclude that Balbus is the sole author of the letter and that Oppius included his name only in order to declare his assent with the content of the words") (*Über die Sprache der Epistolographen S. Supicius Galba und L. Cornelius Balba* [Wurzburg: H. Sturtz, 1888] 30*)*.
4. *Galatians*, chapter 2.
5. In the *Speaker's Commentary* edited by F. C. Cook and Henry Wace (London: John Murray, 1899).
6. *Cities and Bishoprics of Phrygia*, 2.711, 723.

Chapter Five

1. Henry Alford, *Greek New Testament* (Grand Rapids: Guardian Press, [1875] 1976) 2.491; Prolegomena 49.
2. Such is the interpretation of that difficult passage advocated in

Galatians, chapter 9. I should now say that the interpretation gives the thought which was implicit in the mind of Paul, but which was not expressed by him explicitly to the Galatians, though now it is fully stated to the Corinthians. The interpretation of the American revisers, towards which I indicated a leaning, must be adopted: it contains in embryo the same thought which is matured in this passage of 1 Corinthians.

3. Of course, in 1:13 we must understand that in the question, "Was Paul crucified for you?" we have to take Paul merely as the first of the list, and to add in thought the others—"Was Paul, or Apollos, or Cephas crucified for you?"

Chapter Seven

1. Horace, *Epistles* I.106–7, translation by Conington.
2. 1 Corinthians 8:1ff., as excellently interpreted by Professor W. Lock; see *Expositor* (July 1897) 67, 73.
3. The Revised Version is much inferior here to the Authorized Version.
4. *St. Paul the Traveller,* 149.

Chapter Eight

1. The letters of the younger Pliny about his uncle show us a thoroughly conscientious, hardworking, and humane officer; and the fact that he was far from brilliant intellectually makes him all the better a representative of the average.
2. This is one main thought of *The Church in the Roman Empire.*
3. The son of a freedman was *ingenuus*, and free from many of the disabilities of his slave-born sire; the grandson of a freedman was free from all disabilities, and could rise to all *honores* in the state. (Claudius introduced a stricter rule, but did not maintain it; see Suetonius, *Claudius* 24). This was true only of the most representative classes of freedmen, namely, those set free by the most complete and legal methods, *vindicta,* etc.
4. Such seems a fair account of the theory underlying Augustus' institution of the *Seviri Augustales.*
5. That is, the ears of one who has been a slave, but who is now marked by the *praenomen* as free (Horace, *Satires* 2.5.33).
6. In Asia Minor a name like Gaius or Lucius was often assumed by a provincial as his single name of the Greek fashion. In such cases Gaius or Lucius is no longer a *praenomen*, but has become a non-Roman name. That custom was, however, not common in Greece at this time, but belonged rather to the less educated cities.
7. So Ludwig Friedländer, *Cena Trimalchionis* (Leipzig: S. Hirzel, 1891) 7. Some place the scene under Augustus or Tiberius. On the name Gaius, see Friedländer, p. 207.
8. There are certain dangers, liable always to arise from the predominance of this "middle" class; and these can perhaps be observed in this letter.

Chapter Nine

1. See *Galatians,* chapter 2.
2. Macedonia, where also women occupied a higher position than in

Greece, is out of the question, because in that case the agents would rather travel between Corinth and a Macedonian harbor.

Chapter Ten

1. *St. Paul the Traveller*, 218–24.
2. Taken alone, the failure of the Greek form (necessarily rare in our authorities) would be unimportant.
3. *St. Paul the Traveller*, 259.
4. Corinth is doubtful (see preceding paragraph), but should probably be added to the list, if we are right in discrediting the authority of the great manuscripts in Acts 18:17 and believing that the Received Text is nearer the truth.

Chapter Eleven

1. For example, marriages between parent and child, or between brother and sister. Eusebius and Basil speak very emphatically about these customs in eastern Asia Minor, and I have pointed out various facts bearing on this in the *Quarterly Review* (October 1897) 425–26.
2. When one asks for proof of the statement (made in many books on Greek antiquities) that such a marriage would have offended Greek feeling, one finds that the proof reduces itself to this passage of Paul—misunderstood, as we contend.
3. It is pointed out in *Galatians*, section 17, that Rome did not try or desire to destroy existing civilization and law by forcing her own on the Greek cities. Rome made it a rule to "let well alone."
4. But marriage between an uncle and his sister's daughter was never allowed by Roman law nor between a nephew and aunt.

Chapter Twelve

1. φυσιοῦμαὶ, 4:6, 18, 19; 5:2; 8:1; 13:4.
2. καύχημα, καυχάομαι, καύχησις, 34 times in Corinthians; 16 times in all the rest of the Pauline epistles.
3. See the quotations and remarks in chapter 7.
4. *Galatians,* chapter 45.

Chapter Thirteen

1. They are doubtless meant as κυβερνεήσεις (12:28), προιστάμενοι in 1 Thessalonians 5:12 (ἡγούμενοι is not Pauline).

Chapter Fourteen

1. To bring out the distinction of σὺν τῇ δυνάμει from the usual ἐν δυνάμει, which would imply acting " in and with the power of God."
2. Quoted from Henry Alford's note on 2 Corinthians 9:1 (*Greek Testament* [Grand Rapids: Guardian, (1877) 1976] 2.685, where he refers in illustration to the sentence now before us. Compare Meyer-Heinriei, "das μέν solitarium ist zu fassen: ich wenigstens" ("the μέν *solitarium* expresses: At least I").
3. Alford, *Greek Testament*, 2.506.
4. παραχωρεῖν τῇ θεῷ the goddess is often mentioned instead of the god in these inscriptions, but we need not observe the distinction of sex.

5. This class of invocation passes by insensible steps into the class of magical *devotiones*, consigning one's enemies to the gods of death. The essential difference between these classes is that in one the god is invoked to avenge real injury, in the other to gratify personal spite. That is a real and serious difference, and was recognized in ancient times, the latter class being illicit and secret. Yet it is impossible to say where one ends and the other beings.
6. Some account of this interesting class of "confessions" is given in "The Greek of the Early Church and the Pagan Ritual" in *Expository Times* (October 1898–January 1899).

Chapter Fifteen

1. The date in the autumn of the preceding year (*St. Paul the Traveller*, p. 275) is erroneous. The two epistles were not separated by so long an interval as that dating would require. Paul, when once his attention was directed to the unsatisfactory state of the Corinthian church, never relaxed his efforts (see also chapter 16).
2. The rendering of verses 9 and 11 in the Revised Version seems correct. It takes the aorist in verse 9 as referring to the old letter, and in verse 11 to the new; but this harshness is mitigated by the context (especially νῦν) and the general sense of the passage.

Chapter Sixteen

1. Titus was making the coasting voyage from Corinth to Troas along the Macedonian shores, and hence Paul could count on meeting him all the sooner if he sailed along the coast in the opposite direction.
2. This is implied by "contrariwise" and "the more" (marginal reading rightly) in 2 Corinthians 2:6–7.
3. *St. Paul the Traveller*, 234.

Chapter Seventeen

1. It is not till chapter 7 that Paul takes up the questions laid before him by the Corinthians, though he had always in mind their words and arguments in chapters 1–6.
2. Charles John Ellicott, *St. Paul's First Epistle to the Corinthians* (London: Longmans, Green, 1887) ad loc.
3. τὸν ἕτερον, another of the same species or class, therefore a fellow Christian, a good example of the strict sense of ἕτερος, contended for in *Galatians*, chapter 11. For an example (in addition to those there quoted) of the same distinction between ἕτερος, "a second of the same class," and ἄλλος, "belonging to a different class," see Demosthenes' *Olynthiae* 3:18 (where Dr. Sandys has the note, ἄλλος, "anyone else," in general, ἕτερος, "a second speaker"). I am indebted to Mr. A. Souter for the quotation.
4. Modern commentators rightly reject, though in a somewhat hesitating way, the rendering that βιωτικά means "matters of this life," "secular," as distinguished from "matters of the other world" (implied, on that view, by the reference to judging angels); βιωτικά means "trivial," "commonplace" (Luke 21:34).
5. τούτους καθίζετε does not mean "make these (permanent official) judges," but "set these as arbitrators in the various cases, as they

arise." Those commentators who hold that courts of arbitration among the Christians are here counseled, speak of such courts as if they were a purely Jewish institution. But Paul is not here trying to induce the Greeks to accept a Jewish custom; he is referring to the ordinary Greek usage, only advising them to choose a Christian as an arbitrator in each case.

6. Rendered "extortion" in 2 Corinthians 9:5 ("covetousness" in the margin).
7. *Galatians*, section 19.
8. There is a great lack of evidence about such matters in eastern *coloniae*; but the above statement gives the probable fact; cf. *Galatians*, section 19.

Chapter Nineteen

1. Follow the marginal translation of the Revised Version, taking καθίζετε as an imperative.

Chapter Twenty

1. It is hard to see why Canon Evans and several other commentators should insist that ἐλούσασθε cannot mean "washed yourselves," but must be rendered "washed away your sins." One can understand that the Corinthian Christians "washed themselves," but it is not easy to see how any but divine power could be said to "wash away their sins." That λούομαι means *lavo me, lavor* is a general belief of scholars, and rule in lexicons; and even Canon Evans, excellent scholar as he was, cannot by a mere dictum unsupported by proofs overturn it.
2. Wherever Paul says "you know" or "do you not know?" the Corinthians would be reminded of their claim to possess universal knowledge.
3. In all the great centers of travel and trade, the same results were likely to be produced in an age when every inn was also practically a house of ill-fame, but that state of things lasted into late medieval times.

Chapter Twenty-One

1. καλὸν ἀνθρώπῳ γυναικὸς μὴ ἅπτεσθαὶ.
2. καὶ ὁ γαμίζων τὴν παρθένον ἑαυτοῦ καλῶς ποιεῖ καὶ ὁ μὴ γαμίζων κρεῖσσον ποιήσεὶ.
3. ἐὰν δὲ κοιμηθῇ ὁ ἀνήρ, ἐλευθέρα ἐστὶν ᾧ θέλει γαμηθῆναι, μόνον ἐν κυρίῳ μακαριωτέρα δέ, ἐστιν ἐὰν οὕτως μείνῃ, κατὰ τὴν ἐμὴν γνώμην, δοκῶ δὲ κἀγὼ πνεῦμα θεοῦ ἔχειὺ.
4. See *Galatians*, chapter 54.
5. *Lex Julia* in 18 B.C., repeated in severer form as *Lex Papia Poppea*.
6. Marriage was a condition, undoubtedly, for the priesthood in the imperial cultus: man and wife were appointed high priest and high priestess, as is shown by many inscriptions.

Chapter Twenty-Two

1. Canon Evans rightly sees that 7:6 refers only to the custom alluded to in 7:5. It is an unfortunate result of the prevalent misapprehension of the question discussed by Paul, that many interpreters take 7:6 to mean, "I permit, but am far from enjoining, marriage." Canon Evans,

though sharing that misapprehension, felt the inevitable sequence of thought between the two verses 5 and 6, as everyone must to whom Greek has become a living tongue. Could we hear Paul read aloud his letter, the tone of voice would permit no doubt on the connection and the sense.

Chapter Twenty-Three

1. According to the two theories, which alone are possible as to Paul's condition: either he was a widower or he had never married.

Chapter Twenty-Four

1. Here, as before, all attempts to deduce from the personal reference evidence whether Paul was a widower or celibate rest on misunderstanding.

Chapter Twenty-Five

1. Compare *Galatians*, chapter 40.
2. Compare *Galatians*, chapter 31.
3. *Galatians*, sections 5, 19; *Church in the Roman Empire,* 397–98.
4. This is not inconsistent with their weakness as a lawmaking and law-abiding race. Where they failed was not in disinclination to law, but in unwillingness to accept law imposed from without. The individual right to be a law to himself was too much emphasized in the Greek mind. Even the law of the city was liable to seem an outrage on the freedom of each individual to carry out his own conception of order and law.
5. This view was the natural development in the Jewish mind. As Israel Abrahams says: "The Scriptures had used the relation of husband to wife as a type of God's relation to His world. Jewish mystics of the Middle Ages compared a man's love to God with a man's love for his wife" (*Jewish Life in the Middle Ages* [London: Macmillan, 1896] 86). Probably no one that has any true sympathy with the Oriental mind could doubt that the Song of Solomon is an allegory, though the Western mind can hardly see it.
6. Did St. Paul conceive the analogy as perfect? Was the church to him the complement of Christ, essential to the realization of His nature?
7. *Galatians*, chapter 63.
8. See *Galatians*, chapter 54.
9. See Professor Findlay's restoration of their letter in the *Expositor* (June 1900) 404; see also the *Expositor* (April 1900) 287–88.
10. On these suspicions see, for example, chapter 6 of Edward William Lane's *Manners and Customs of the Modern Egyptians* (London: J. M. Dent, 1908).

Chapter Twenty-Six

1. Lane, *Manners and Customs.*
2. *Jewish Life in the Middle Ages*, pp. 91, 131.
3. He quotes the words in his article "Marriage," Hastings' *Dictionary of the Bible* (Peabody, MA: Hendrickson, [1898] 1988) 3.266.
4. On the charge of Sadduceeism brought against Paul, there is much to say which needs a paper to itself.

Chapter Twenty-Seven

1. See *Cities and Bishoprics of Phrygia*, 2.491ff. *Agape* may yet be discovered in a pagan inscription, as Sozomene has been at Blaundos; see Karl Buresch, *Aus Lydien* (Leipzeig: B. G. Teubner, 1898) 120.
2. "Apollos...rendered us welcome and fruitful service after your departure...Happily at your request he will come again to Corinth and resume his work among us: this we earnestly desire and entreat" (*Expositor* [June 1900] 403).
3. As Mr. C. F. Andrews, Pembroke College, Cambridge, points out, Galatians 3:1 and 6:11 show the same thought burning in Paul's mind and guiding his expression. Formerly he had "placarded" Christ before their eyes. Now he takes the pen, at the end of the letter, to placard before them in "big striking letters" the main thoughts of the preceding chapters. In a sense he was not above "advertising" his gospel. He chooses that word to express his method: προγράφω is literally to advertise, προγραφή, an advertisement, and they are used, for example, of advertising a sale, a meeting, the business of a public assembly, etc. In ancient times advertisement by multiplication of small copies was not possible, only by announcements posted in a prominent place where they would be readily seen by many people.

Chapter Twenty-Eight

1. I regret to see Professor Findlay (*1 Corinthians*, EGT, 2.839) rejects the translation of 8:2, "we know that we all have knowledge," as tautologous, and renders "we know, because we all have knowledge." The tautology lies only in the wrong use of one English term, know and knowledge, to translate two very distinct Greek terms, οἶδα and γνῶσις. The meaning really is, "we know that we all possess the power of discerning truth."
2. EGT, 2.336; the quote is from F. J. A. Hort, *The Christian Ecclesia* (London: Macmillan, 1897) 88–89.
3. *St. Paul the Traveller*, p. 172.

Chapter Twenty-Nine

1. *St. Paul the Traveller*, pp. 121–22.
2. This is fully conceded by Professor Findlay (*1 Corinthians*, EGT, 2.849); and he is one of the scholars who maintain most positively that Paul had refrained from appointing any officers at Corinth (cf. 2.732; 2.950).
3. See the following note. There has been much dispute as to the character of the *gerousia* in cities of Asia Minor. It varied to some extent, in some places having more of an official character, in others being more purely social; see Lévy, in *Revue des Études Grecque* (1895) 231ff.; W. Liebenan, *Stadteverwaltung im römischen Kaiserreiche* (Leipzig: Duncker & Humblot, 1900) 565; D. G. Hogarth in *Journal of Philology*, 19.70ff.; Ramsay, *Cities and Bishoprics Of Phrygia*, 1.111; E. Ziebarth, *Das griechische Vereinswesen* (Leipzig: S. Hirzel, 1896) 131.
4. The relation of the Christian usage of *presbyteros* to local expression has not escaped Professor Deissmann, who treats it at some length in

his *Bible Studies* (Peabody, Mass.: Hendrickson, [1901] 1988) 154–57, 233–35. He points out that official *presbyteroi* are often mentioned in Egypt and in Asia Minor. One desiderates in his remarks (as often throughout his admirable and suggestive studies) a livelier sense of the quality of Greek expression, and a perception of the fact that persons who wrote and spoke Greek of a higher and more cultured style would avoid the term. He also points out, what I have omitted above, that the term *proëgoumenos* was applied to the president of the *presbyteroi* or *geraioi* in some parts of Asia Minor.

5. See Acts 20:17, 28, confirmed by 1 Timothy 3:17. There can be no reasonable doubt that Timothy was addressed as being in a kind of charge over the Asian churches.
6. See *Cities and Bishoprics of Phrygia*, 2.520, 548. *Geraios* in Eumenea has as yet been found only in Christian inscriptions, but may possibly denote only the members of the city *gerousia*. The inscription of Hierapolis mentioning the *proëdria* still seems to me Jewish-Christian; but I was wrong in making the Porphyrabaphoi a Christian guild. They were a Jewish society, and hence Christianity had a strong footing among them.
7. In Acts 15:22 *hegoumenoi* occurs, but it is evidently merely quoted.
8. *St. Paul the Traveller*, pp. 267–68.
9. 1 Clement 1.3 uses the term about the Corinthian officers (while he mentions *presbyteroi* only as elderly and reverend men), and the name was also used at Jerusalem (Acts 15:22). The term used in the Roman church was *proëgoumenoi* (1 Clement 21.6; Hermas 6.6; 17.7; *hegoumenoi* in 1 Clement 37.3 refers to imperial government officials). It is therefore quite marvelous that the occurrence of *hegoumenoi* in Hebrews should be appealed to by Harnack and others as a proof that that epistle was addressed, not to Jerusalem, but to Rome. So far as it proves anything, it proves the very opposite.

Chapter Thirty

1. *The Church in the Roman Empire before 170*, pp. 364–71.

Chapter Thirty-One

1. For my own part I regard this as practically certain; and Dr. Ziebarth, *Das griechische Vereinswesen*, p. 211, points out that many of them became of a character not unlike "clubs" in modern English life.
2. The evidence about most of them is confined to one or two references in each case. In many cases we know nothing except the name.
3. See Ziebarth, ibid., p. 196.
4. Professor Findlay in his reconstruction of their letter puts it thus (*Expositor* [June 1900] 403): "We must depart from Corinth: nay, we doubt whether in the whole world we should find any spot where men dwell that is clear of defilement." One would only wish that he had not restricted this by his context to the one department of personal chastity. Probably the Corinthians either meant it in a much wider sense, or used a similar expression more than once, explaining that they could hardly avoid intercourse with idolators unless they were to "go out of the world" (see 5:10).

Chapter Thirty-Two

1. ἐκ τυμπανου βέβρωκα, ἐκ κυμβάλου πέπωκα: Firmicus Maternus (*On the Error of Profane Religions*) and Clement of Alexandria (*Protrepticus* 2): literally, the holy drum and cymbal of the goddess. The authorities differ a little as to the words. Firmicus finishes γέγονα μύστης Αττεως.
2. The term *symbiosis* described the club on its nonreligious side, but was also applicable to a religious association. The religious and non-religious sides of the clubs melted into one another, and cannot be distinguished sharply.
3. Ziebarth, *Das griechische Vereinswesen*, pp. 52, 206; ὁι συμβιοταὶ καὶ συμμύσται, under the common article.
4. Ziebarth, ibid., p. 211.

Chapter Thirty-Three

1. *Galatians*, section 9.

Chapter Thirty-Four

1. See Hermann C. Maue's treatise, *Der Praefectus Fabrum* (Halle: Niemeyer, 1887) 27; most of this paragraph is simply abbreviated from him.
2. Maue, ibid., repeats that wrong statement. See M. Rostovtzeff in *Revue Numismatique* (1898) 282–83. Nero dissolved certain clubs in Pompeii, but that was because they had misdirected their fellowship and aims and had fostered disorder (Tacitus, *Annals* 4.17).
3. See Maue, ibid., p. 31.
4. See *Galatians*, chapters 17ff. and 23ff.
5. This guidance was what Paul feared (1 Cor. 11:21; below, chapter 37).
6. Although the origin of this name is unknown, its connotation is clear: the Nicolaitans claimed the right to remain in ordinary pagan society and to continue to be members of the clubs.
7. *Cities and Bishoprics of Phrygia*, 2.502–8; see also *Contemporary Review* (September 1896) 435ff.

Chapter Thirty-Five

1. "The blessing" from the first institution still accompanies it.
2. I had the advantage of discussing 1 Corinthians 8 and 10 for several days with my friend Professor Sayce in the end of October. The run of the thought long puzzled us. With his usual insight he pointed out that the heart of the question lay in the "communion of *daimonia*, 10:20." When at last the suggestion was made that the sacrificial meal of the *thiasoi* was meant, everything seemed to us to become clear forthwith.

Chapter Thirty-Six

1. εἰς θλῖψιν does not correspond to εἰς κλίνην: εἰς has a different but quite usual sense in each case. I throw her on a couch and her partners beside her (on their couches), with a view to (give them) much suffering.

2. ἀνέπεσεν in Luke 22:14; ἀνέκειτο in Matthew 26:20; and so in Luke 22:27, ἀνακείμενος (cf. Mark 14:18; 16:14). John uses both words freely.

Chapter Thirty-Seven

1. The name is used for brevity's sake, without implying a theory. As in the *Church in the Roman Empire*, p. 492 (in later editions), I still think that the epistle was written by a follower of St. Peter (even more full of Roman ideas than the author of 1 Peter), who considered that he was expressing Peter's opinions. It is not impossible that this may have been done under Peter's own instructions. I am disposed to think that the epistle is earlier than I formerly allowed; see below.
2. We take δόξας as a rendering of *honores*, offices—positions of authority and trust in the church.
3. In the following phrase, if we read with the great manuscripts ἀδικούμενοι μισθὸν ἀδικίας, the only reasonable sense seems to be "deprived (after all) of the way of their wrongdoing." They bargained for certain pay, and are cheated of it. The Revised Version, "suffering wrong as the hire of their wrongdoing," seems self-contradictory, for they are not said to suffer wrong, but to suffer right.
4. The practice of beginning to feast in the daytime is often alluded to by Roman writers either as the extreme of unprincipled luxury (see Juvenal, 1:103, *ab octava Marius bibit* [*hora*]), or as a pardonable stretch of liberty on a holiday (Horace, *Odes* 3.3, *partem solido demere de die*).
5. σπῖλος like Latin *macula*.
6. The scathing picture of a *komos*, a drunken revel, as it is shown in Greek vase pictures and in literature, cannot be mistaken; see *Galatians*, chapter 51.
7. From *The Church in the Roman Empire*, p. 246, where the context states the principle more fully.
8. Ibid., pp. 296–97.
9. *St. Paul the Traveller,* p. 149.

Chapter Thirty-Eight

1. That the communion of the sacrament is in Paul's mind in 6:17 is clear from what has been said in chapters 32 and 33.

Chapter Thirty-Nine

1. This remark also applies to the second Corinthian epistle, in which these halts and fresh starts are so obvious that they have attracted much attention; and some scholars have been led to the erroneous idea that the parts have been put together in the wrong order; or rather, that the epistle is not a single letter written in parts at intervals, but contains two or more distinct letters, of which the one now placed last was written first. Against this theory we believe that 2 Corinthians was a letter, sent to Corinth as it has come down to us, but that considerable intervals elapsed between the composition of the parts.
2. Thus the thoughts of πορνεία and εἰδωλολατρεία tend to pass into one another.

Chapter Forty

1. Some say a year or two earlier or later. All are agreed that the season of the year lay within those limits.

Chapter Forty-One

1. 3:10; 4:15, 16, 21; 7:7, 8, 40; 8:13; 9:1ff.; 10:33; 11:1, 2, 34; 14:18; 15:1ff., 31, etc.; also the frequent "I order, I give my judgment," etc.
2. See, for example, Sabine Baring-Gould's *Study of St. Paul* (London: Isbister, 1897) 206, 263.
3. For example, by Professor Findlay in the *Expositor* (June 1900) 402.

Chapter Forty-Three

1. πολλοὺς παιδαγωγούς (4:15); see *Galatians*, chapter 39: the sentence in the final paragraph, which (as is there said) "may perhaps be fanciful," seems now to me to be so.
2. *The Church in the Roman Empire*, pp. 429–32.
3. It is needless to point out how well all this would suit the Gaius of Romans 16:23, "my host and (host) of the whole church" in Corinth, on the great route between the East and Rome. The name, however, was a common one.

Chapter Forty-Four

1. ἔπεμψα, an epistolary aorist; in English it ought to be expressed by a present.
2. See Professor Rendel Harris's paper on "Epaphroditus, Scribe and Courier" in the *Expositor* (December 1898) 401ff.
3. See the preceding note. Timothy did not go on to Corinth until he accompanied Paul thither. Paul found him still in Macedonia (*St. Paul the Traveller*, p. 276).
4. One sees numerous cases in which the envoys of cities (πρέσβεις) in this period did the same. Persons were often selected as *presbeis* either in order to give them the opportunity of visiting Rome, or because they were going to Rome on their own business.
5. *St. Paul the Traveller*, p. 284 (at the foot of the page read "winter or spring" instead of "autumn").
6. In 2 Corinthians 2:12 the perfects ἀνεῳγμένης and ἔσχηκα, "though a door has been opened unto me, I have found no relief," prove this. The epistolary tense, ἐξῆλθον ἀποταξάμενος, is used of his departure from Troas.
7. In the *Commentary on the Bible* edited by Rev. F. C. Cook (1881).

Chapter Forty-Five

1. In doing so we follow chiefly Canon Evans's admirable edition, and often use his words.
2. The Authorized Version places only a comma here, and makes verse 4 the continuation of the sentence. The Revised Version rightly puts a period. There is a distinct pause at this point after verses 1–3, which form a closely connected whole. Alford and Evans seem right in this (so too Findlay, etc.). The punctuation in Westcott and Hort's text places the pause at the end of verse 2 and connects verse 3 with the

following verses, though marking it off by a period. That view is susceptible of defense; but Canon Evans's view carries conviction.

3. The last passage refers to a different incident, which as an "ecstatic vision" is regarded by some (following Neander) as much less important. Paul himself recognizes no such distinction of dignity, but counts those visions as the greatest glory of his life.
4. *Galatians*, chapter 12.
5. *St. Paul the Traveller*, p. 67.

Chapter Forty-Six

1. More strictly "slave," under the dominion of another man or men.
2. This is not wholly forgotten in Galatians; see 5:13.
3. See *Galatians*, chapter 54.
4. The same thought, of course, occurs in Galatians 3:28.
5. The second half of the verse is enigmatic. It has been understood by Alford and others as "if you are even able to become free, remain in slavery rather"; but (although this is quite possible with the Greek) we feel bound to conclude with Evans and Findlay that Paul means, "but still, if you can also become free, rather make use of the opportunity (than not)." Though Alford's construction is in keeping with the general tone of the context, yet we scruple to take such an extreme meaning. Paul seems to be making a concession parenthetically in spite of the context.

Chapter Forty-Seven

1. On the emphatic position assigned to Cephas, as marking a climax, see the next chapter.
2. Hence κατὰ ἄνθρωπον in the following verse; so *Galatians*, chapter 33.
3. The Greek armies of the later centuries B.C. were indeed largely mercenary; but the idea always remained as a theory in the Greek city that every citizen of suitable age is a soldier in case of need.

Chapter Forty-Eight

1. *Galatians*, chapters 3 and 4.
2. See Lightfoot's note on Clement in the *Apostolic Fathers* (Peabody, MA: Hendrickson [1891] 1994) 2.26.
3. Lucan, *Navig*, describes an Alexandrian corn ship on its way to Rome as lying in the harbor of Piraeus, not far from Corinth; but it is evident that the visit was an unusual and unnatural episode of such a voyage, introduced for the sake of this dialogue, and explained as due to bad winds.

Chapter Forty-Nine

1. Peter also would not cross the sea in winter, and could therefore not reach Corinth earlier than late spring in 54.
2. *Usque ad principium Neroniani imperii*, chapter 2.
3. *Cumque iam Nero imperaret Petrus Romam advenit:* the *iam* implies *principium Neroniani imperii.*
4. *Der Todestage der Apostel Paulus und Petrus und ihre römischen Denkmaler* (Leipzig: J. C. Hinrichs, 1899) 13–14.

5. *Petrus ingressus in urbe Roma Nerone Cesare I.*, that is, A.D. 55.

Chapter Fifty

1. ὤφθην σοι, in Acts 26:16 and 1 Corinthians 15:8, is quite adequately rendered in the Revised Version by "appeared to you." The Authorized Version has "was seen" in 1 Corinthians and "appeared to you" in Acts. For perfect accuracy we need "appeared to your sight," an awkward phrase.
2. ὧν τε εἶδες (v. 16) in the immense majority of manuscripts, including ℵ A (but not B C), is defended by 22:15, μάρτυς . . . ὧν ἑώρακας καὶ ἤκουσας, and is rightly preferred by almost all modern editors (Tischendorf, Blass, Knowling, Meyer-Wendt, Baljou, etc.). Westcott-Hort and Rendall follow B C, ὧν τε εἶδες με, but the construction then is worse than rude; it is intolerable in a speaker like Paul. We can understand him being led on in a desire for balance and symmetry to add ὧν τε ὀφθήσομαί σοι after μάρτυρα ὧν τε εἶδες, but not his saying μάρτυρα ὧν τε εἶδες μη. The corruption arose through the straining after a supposed correspondence εἶδες μη with ὀφθήσομαί σοι.
3. Beyond doubt Luke thought it unnecessary to relate that Ananias delivered the message. He tells of the message given to Ananias, and then of the meeting between Ananias and Saul. The rest is left to be inferred by the reader.
4. Acts 26:17 and 20 furnish a good example of the general principle we are trying to illustrate. In verse 17 Paul is commissioned to the Gentiles; but in verse 20 he goes, in obedience to the heavenly vision, to the people of Damascus, Jerusalem, and Judea, "and also to the Gentiles," showing conclusively that the vision gave him a general commission to all people, Jews and Gentiles.